MW00717538

Coudersport Glass

1900–1904

By Tulla Majot

With Paul W. Heimel

Photography by
David Richardson

Additional Photography by Curt Weinhold

basal text: Times New Roman
display type: Garamond Bold Condensed

Antique Publications
A Division of The Glass Press, Inc.

ISBN 1-57080-067-7 (PB)
ISBN 1-57080-068-5 (HB)

The Glass Press, Inc.
P.O. Box 553 • Marietta, Ohio 45750-0553

first printing: United States of America

Dedication

Robert K. Currin

This book would not have been possible without the assistance and guidance of Robert K. Currin, long-time curator of the Potter County Historical Society Museum in Coudersport, Pennsylvania.

My teacher when I arrived in Coudersport as a child, my tutor when I was recovering from an injury, and my friend as I reached adulthood, Bob Currin has been one constant in my life.

Because of Bob's passion for local history and my own keen interest in Coudersport Glass, our paths converged in 1982 for a public presentation that we have repeated and expanded again and again. This book is a logical extension of that effort.

A retired social studies teacher and school administrator, a devoted grandfather and a long-time caretaker of local history, Bob Currin prefers to keep a low profile; he avoids public recognition at every opportunity. At the same time, Bob is always eager to share his knowledge of the people and places of north-central Pennsylvania with anyone who has the time and the inclination to learn.

Contents

Acknowledgments

Research and Writing

This book has been several years in the making. During that time I have been blessed with the help of many people. As I began the research, many doors were opened for me and many people shared their knowledge with me.

First and foremost is Bob Currin, curator of the Potter County Historical Society Museum. Bob's vast knowledge of the history of Coudersport and Potter County has been a never-ending source of information for me. His wonderful memory about the origin of the Coudersport Glass donated to the museum has also served me well. Bob also authored an abbreviated history that served as a foundation for this larger work.

Frank Fenton at the Fenton Art Glass Company in Williamstown, West Virginia, opened all of his files and made both my husband and me feel welcome and comfortable while using these facilities. He also was very informative about his father's involvement in the Coudersport plant. Researcher Berry Wiggins shared his notes and resources with me, and helped us sort through the Fenton files.

Jim Measell shared his notes about Webb & Bastow and offered many suggestions for sources to be investigated. Jim very kindly reviewed one of the first drafts of this history for accuracy, and provided helpful suggestions.

The women in the research department of Rakow Library in Corning, New York, were extremely helpful and saved me hours of work. Serious glass researchers are aware of how fortunate we are to have these catalogs and trade magazines on microfilm in this wonderful library.

My good friends Betty Cooney and Andrea Turton helped me dig for information at Corning. Andrea also prepared the first comprehensive timeline from bits and pieces of my notes.

The *Potter Enterprise* newpaper files were at my disposal and many of the news articles came from that publication as well as the *Potter County Journal*. Carl Roberts combed through the newspaper files at the library one last time and located some missing links that included information about the delinquent taxes.

This book would never have become a reality without the skills of two of Coudersport's most talented people.

Paul Heimel assisted me in evaluating the assembled information and putting it in readable form. Paul—an author and former newspaper editor—was the logical person to assist in the compilation of this history. Paul is always very busy between his sportscasting job, raising a family and being active in the community. When I asked him for help, he took on the project wholeheartedly.

For layout of this book I turned to my son, Joseph A. Majot. As publisher of the *Potter-Leader Enterprise*, he is experienced in newspaper layout as well as book design. I asked him to share his considerable talents with me to set this (my first and last) book in a style with which we both felt comfortable.

To all of those people mentioned here, and to the many others involved, I owe my heartfelt thanks. Without your help this book would never have been completed.

Acknowledgments

Glass and Photography

Several years ago, I asked local photographer Curt Weinhold to begin photographing my collection of Coudersport Glass. At the time, the idea was to produce a complete set of prints showing the glassware that had been authenticated as Coudersport.

Through the help of Bob Currin, we were also able to photograph pieces from the Potter County Historical Society Museum that I did not have.

Curt Weinhold is a true professional, as well as a real perfectionist. Working with glassware was a new experience for him. He went out of his way to experiment with different backgrounds, angles and arrangements of the glass to produce some very unique photographs.

Curt also visited the home of my good friends Carl and Linda Roberts, to photograph their fireplaces which contain tile from the local plant. Other friends loaned Stock certificates for photography. The Webb certificate belongs to Paul and Delores Buchsen, and the Bastow certificate to Bob and Anona Green. Thanks to these generous people, these pieces of history are now recorded for future generations.

Other Coudersport residents had pieces that were different from mine or the museum's. It is with a strong sense of small town pride that I can say no one ever refused to share these with me. Thus, we are able to present a section of photography that is as complete as humanly possible.

Of particular help were Paul and Delores Buchsen, and Rayburn (Jaybird) and Esther Weimer. Time and again, I have gone back and asked for the use of a specific piece. Thank you for your trust in me; you will never know how much I worried about your things while I had them in my possession.

The beautiful Communion Set was provided for photography courtesy of The Seventh Day Adventist Church in Coudersport, and Jackie Dehn and Scott Bruzzi also entrusted some beautiful pieces to me.

Other glass items were brought to the museum for one last photo session courtesy of Mina Cooney, Ed Darrin, Jackie Dehn, Marty Fry, Shirlee Leete, Curtis and Janice Nelson, John Peet, and Jim and Penny Thomas.

Photography at the final session was taken by Dave Richardson, publisher of this book. Dave and I want to thank Linda Roberts, Janice and Curtis Nelson, my daughter Ginny Kio and my husband Joe, for their help with unpacking and repacking glass, and keeping straight the ownership of each item. This allowed us to complete the work in only three days. A special thank you, Janice, for cleaning the cases.

I cannot thank everyone enough for all of your generosity, help and encouragement. This book may carry my byline but it is really a joint effort of my family and friends and the collectors mentioned above.

Webb Patent Tile Co. and Joseph Webb Decorative Glass Co. 1900-1901

*For of all sad words of
tongue and pen, the saddest are these:
'It might have been!'*

—John Greenleaf Whittier

No one alive today was an eyewitness to the facilities that brought the world a product that has come to be known as "Coudersport Glass." Instead, we are left to piece together many diverse fragments from that all-too-brief period of time when a handful of notable and talented glassmakers crossed paths in a tiny community nestled in the hills of north-central Pennsylvania.

The talents, energies and aspirations of the Webb family from England, as well as Harry Bastow and the Fentons from the United States, played a major role in the production of what we now call Coudersport Glass. It is named after the small community where they made their respective bids to compete in a volatile marketplace, suffered severe setbacks, and moved on. Fire would roar through the glass plant just when it appeared to be on the brink of some major advances, destroying the hopes and dreams of hundreds who believed the facility was destined for great things. Those rare collectibles that surface from time to time today in yard sales and antique auctions only tease us to speculate about "what might have been."

Through a variety of colors, shapes and styles, each piece reflects the hopes and dreams of an optimistic era. The premium pieces portray a distinct beauty and attention to detail not often found in today's mass-produced household glass. Other remnants tell us that the producers recognized the importance of appealing to the mass market, thus fulfilling their pledge to produce a variety of blown and molded glass "suitable to the cottage or the mansion."

While production of Coudersport Glass took place over a span of nearly five years (1900–1904), the actual manufacturing was sporadic. The plant stood dormant for months at a time, the victim of economic setbacks and marketplace miscalculations that forced the owners to return to the drawing board and retool on several occasions. One can only speculate as to the motivations and aspirations of Joseph Webb, Frank L. Fenton, Harry Bastow, or any of the others who committed their time and talents to the products. We are left to piece together a history of the plant based on newspaper clippings, advertisements, photographs and other archives. Further insight can be gained by a thorough, objective assessment of the industrial, economic and social factors of the era.

At the dawn of the 20th century, the vast forests of northcentral Pennsylvania were producing millions of board feet of lumber for the world's market. After the Civil War, land barons began to cash in on the rich stands of native pine and hemlock. As they harvested and processed these resources, an infrastructure was put in place to accommodate both the lumber industry and the growing population that accompanied it. The expanding network of railroads, dirt roads and other public utilities left no doubt that the Allegheny Plateau had been "discovered."

Entire hillsides were denuded as the lumbermen continued their harvest. Certain businesses, from the manufacture of barrel staves and headings to the tanning of leather, were thriving, but community leaders recognized that timber resources were finite. Investors began to look for new industries to fill the void. With an abundance of natural gas—a key factor—as well as rich sandstone resources and ample water supplies, the Coudersport area appeared to be promising for glass manufacturing. The

Lumbermen quickly stripped the Potter County hillsides and moved on. New industries were needed to fill the void.

region also had a large, albeit unskilled, labor force and convenient transportation networks, particularly railroads. America was entering a golden age of glassmaking; jars, bottles and window glass were already being made nearby.

In 1899, after prolonged negotiations, a window glass factory was established on the northern border of Coudersport. About 40 homes were built in close proximity to the American Window Glass Company factory, forming the foundation of a neighborhood now known locally as "Rubbertown" (the result of a truss manufacturing plant that succeeded the glass factory).

American Window Glass Company, which initially employed 95 people, faced economic problems from the outset, due in large part to limitations in the supply of natural gas to keep the furnaces in steady operation. Industry price-fixing, combined with production limits imposed by the monopolistic American Window Glass Trust, made the operation of a small facility such as the Coudersport factory a shaky proposition, at best. Manipulation of both the supply and the price was a standard business practice at the time, necessary for the survival of some industries and not yet prohibited by law.

At about the same time, two members of the famous Webb family, originally from England, were seeking greener pastures in their efforts to corner a greater share of the U.S. market in glass-based tile and ornamental glass.

The Webb name carried a great deal of weight in the glass industry, stemming in large part from the success of the Thomas Webb & Sons Glassworks, a leading producer of colorful, tastefully-decorated tableware and ornamental glass in the coal- and clay-rich region of Stourbridge, England. Two sons of Joseph Webb (1813–1869), a prominent British glassmaker who was the cousin of Thomas Webb, had emigrated to the United States around 1883. The older brother, Joseph Webb (1852–1905), soon made a name for himself in U.S. glasshouses because of his innovations in various yellow and rose-pink glass formulas. His brother, Hugh Fitzroy Webb (1855–1939), focused much of his attention on the production of glass tiles for flooring, roofing, paving, wainscotting, fireplaces and other uses where a durable ornamental substance was desired.

Joseph Webb rose to prominence through his work at the Phoenix Glass Company in West Bridgewater, Pennsylvania. The October 11, 1883, edition of *American Pottery & Glassware Reporter* noted that Joseph Webb "is now superintending the manufacture" of finger bowls and gas shades in "plain and crackled glass of every shade and color— blue, green, amber, canary, lemon, citron, etc."

During a decade of work at the Phoenix facility, Webb obtained patents on his techniques for manufacturing three styles of fancy glassware as well as a lamp globe or shade in 1885. He also registered designs for Ivory finish glass in 1887.

Perhaps attracted by a once-in-a-lifetime opportunity to demonstrate his skills and increase his income, Joseph Webb accepted an offer from the Libbey Glass Company of Toledo, Ohio in March 1893. He helped develop the Libbey exhibit at the 1893 World's Columbian Exposition in Chicago, which included a complete glass factory with 300 employees demonstrating glassmaking.

Within a year, Webb had left Libbey and become affiliated with Dithridge's Fort Pitt Glass Works in Pittsburgh, Pennsylvania. The March 8, 1894 issue of *China, Glass and Lamps* credited Webb with "making some marvelously beautiful things in colored glass" at Fort Pitt. Not coincidentally, that same year Fort Pitt introduced "Rosina," which shaded from deep to light rose.

Trade journals made no reference to Webb again until November 1899, when *China, Glass and Lamps* reported that he was with the Tarentum (Pennsylvania) Glass Company, where he was making a ware "as fine as was ever turned out in the state." The Tarentum firm was known for its opal line called "Georgia," which came in lemon yellow, pomona green and a deep rose-pink.

Meanwhile, H. Fitzroy Webb had been affiliated with Westinghouse Company's glass factory in Greensburg, Pa., but for several years had not been active in the glass trade because of a paralytic stroke.

By late 1899, at least one of the brothers, H. Fitzroy, was seeking a location to produce the ornamental tile on

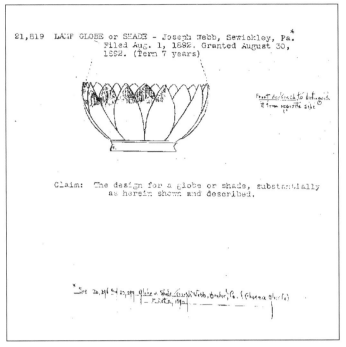

Lamp Globe or Shade patent granted to Joseph Webb, Beaver, PA (Phoenix Glass Co.) August 30, 1892.

which he had been working for some time. At the same time, Coudersport business interests—organized five years earlier as a Board of Trade—were on the lookout for industries to boost the region's prosperity and learned of Webb's interest.

Board of Trade members selected a site on the east

A view of Coudersport from Benson's Hill looking west, circa 1900.

side of Coudersport, less than a mile from the business district, tucked in a narrow valley through which little Mill Creek flows toward its confluence with the Allegheny River. The bulk of this land, consisting of about 150 acres, had been owned for 16 years by Karl and Minnie Zimmerman. An adjacent portion had seen thousands of visitors every year when it was used as a fairgrounds, complete with horse racing and other attractions.

Karl Zimmerman purchased a kiln and began manufacturing bricks just months before he was approached about selling the land.

Negotiations with Webb focused at least in part on the legitimacy of his claim for a patent on the glass tile he proposed to manufacture in Coudersport.

One of the leading promoters of the proposed factory was Luther H. "Lute" Seibert, a Coudersport attorney who was active in Democratic political circles. A colorful character, Seibert raised horses and was one of the first people in Coudersport to purchase an automobile.

Asked by one skeptic what a glass tile factory might do for the town, Lute Seibert replied, "I will have a city here as large as New York or Philadelphia if this thing works out. It is the only glass of its kind made in the world, and we have a cinch on it."

The property changed hands only after protracted negotiations. "The glass tile works Mr. Webb is trying to locate in Coudersport is not so sure," said the Feb. 10, 1900, *Commoner & Glassworker* of Pittsburgh. "The stock has all been subscribed, but there is a hitch on the part of the land owners—some of whom want enormous rates for the land upon which to locate the plant."

H. Fitzroy Webb, who was living in Greensburg, at the time, visited the site and, according to newspaper reports, was pleased with the property and the "inducements offered" by the Board of Trade. Typically, these included free or reduced-price natural gas, plus lots sold by subscription to fund construction of the plant.

The January 3, 1900 edition of the *Potter Enterprise*, one of two weekly newspapers serving the area, reported that prospects were good for the erection of a glass tile factory in Coudersport. H. Fitzroy Webb was identified as one of only four men in the country who thoroughly understood the process for making glass tile, which was seen as a ready sale commodity. He claimed that his product was far superior to anything made by other manufacturers, and said the factory would pay high wages and run at least ten months out of the year.

On January 13, Board of Trade members and other interested parties met once again with Webb to work out details for formation of the Coudersport Glass Tile Plant.

Appearing on the subscription list to buy land from Minnie and Karl Zimmerman were a variety of Coudersport area business owners and other investors: C.H. Armstrong, F.E. Horton, William M. Doud, LeRoy Huff, W. Benson, J.W. Glase, John Heckman, L.A. Glase, Wencil Klesa, C.N. Mattison, W.E. Phelps, C.C. Warren, William VanBuren, D.W. McLaughlin, T.A. Grabe, A.R. Moore, the Underwood Brothers, Garvin & Hitchcock, J.M. Clark, R.B. Knight, Terrance Fee, Milton J. Potter and H.J. Olmsted.

The business plan called for a $50,000 plant that would hire 125 men and support a weekly payroll of $4,000. The tile to be manufactured was of glass about one-fourth inch thick in a wide variety of colors. It was promoted as a less expensive, more attractive and cleaner ornamental building material than wood or stone. Thicker, more durable tile would also be manufactured as market conditions warranted.

Newspaper accounts from the era make repeated references to H. Fitzroy Webb's claim that his tile differed from other glass tile for which other manufacturers held the patent rights.

"Abundant material of excellent quality for manufacture of this tile is at hand in the shape of our sandstone rock which could be obtained at such small cost that the product when put on the market could defy all competition," the other weekly, the *Potter County Journal*, reported.

Sandstone deposits notwithstanding, the plant would need three other important commodities—fuel, water and transportation—to prosper.

Natural gas was the logical choice to fuel the glass melting furnaces, and arrangements were made with the lone vendor, the Potter Gas Company, to provide as steady a supply as could be expected during that era. Construction of a six-inch pipeline from existing distribution routes to the glass factory site would prove to be a major undertaking.

Another major component was the construction of an 1,800-foot siding from the Coudersport & Port Allegany Railroad's eastern spur to the north boundary of the property. Ground transportation was accommodated by U.S Route 6, the "Grand Army of the Republic Highway," a dirt road that served as a major east-west artery for horse-drawn vehicles.

Frank L. Baker, a well-known contractor, was hired to construct a main building measuring 96' by 176', with two wings of 80' by 100' each attached.

On March 2, 1900, the *Potter Enterprise* told its readers, "Work has progressed rapidly until today one of the best-equipped, most modern and well-built factories in the country adorns that which was formerly waste land. The factory ready for manufacturing purposes will cost about $65,000."

On April 4, 1900, the *Potter County Journal* reported, "Progress in construction is slow because of weather. Will have two nine-pot furnaces and one four-ton tank. Seven shops are to be employed blowing the regular window glass tile; there will also be a casting table and a press shop. A writer to a trade paper says H. F. Webb is on the ground and will superintend (completion) of the plant, also manage and make glass."

That same newspaper story addressed the patent issue in great detail:

"He (H. Fitzroy Webb) has the patent of the process by which the glass tile is expected to adhere to the surface desired, instead of fusing on particles of glass as is done by the Opalite Tile Company. He will fuse upon glass with a porous backing which becomes homogenous with the cement with which it is embedded. When asked if he thought that his process interfered with the Opalite Tile Company for which they claim exclusive rights under English patents, he said, 'We have had the highest patent authorities examine their claims and find them untenable. Besides, I think my process is different.'"

The *Potter Enterprise* also addressed the patent issue, lending further credence to the suggestion that it was a major concern even before the first glass tile rolled off the assembly line:

"The tile which will be manufactured at this factory is one of the few patented ones in the world. On its principle it stands entirely alone. There is only one firm in the United States making this class of goods, the Opalite Tile Company of Monaca, Pa. This company purchased the Shelmerding patent of England through a friend of H. Fitzroy Webb which invention is similar to all others as it holds on by a key. The Webb Tile Company (product) has no key but becomes homogenous with the cement and consequently with the wall. There has been a great deal of trouble with the tile placed on the walls with the key system as it becomes loose and falls off after a time, which is a serious drawback to its successful use. The patentee of the Webb Tile Company carefully thought the matter over and came to the conclusion that the principle was not right, thus his invention. There are two or three tiles sold in England which appear to be identically the same as the Shelmerding patent, but the Opalite Tile Company has not taken any action for infringements which seems to be somewhat peculiar."

H. Fitzroy Webb was most likely hedging his bet when

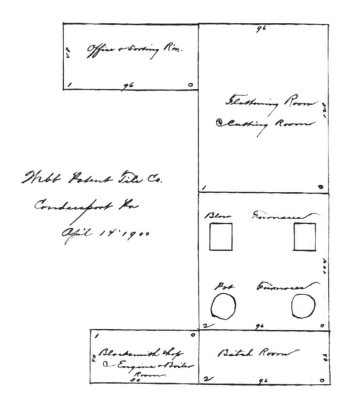

Early layout sketch of the Webb Patent Tile Co. plant.

he revealed that his brother, Joseph Webb, would bring his vast knowledge of ornamental glassmaking to Coudersport. The tile factory, still under construction, would now include a separate division for the production of "fancy glassware," to be known as the Joseph Webb Decorative Glass Company, operating under the same financial structure as the Webb Patent Tile Glass Company. This development boosted the price tag to $65,000.

Original employment forecasts were bumped to 150 people. "Nearly all of the men who will be employed will have to be skilled workmen and therefore can demand high wages," the *Potter Enterprise* reported. "It can therefore be seen that the factory will be of much more benefit to the town than the Window Glass Factory, for the reason that the men will spend all of their time here and will establish homes and become residents. This will probably be a home industry, so this opportunity should meet with every encouragement from those interested in promoting growth and prosperity in our town. Not all profits would accrue to the manufacturer. Every merchant, mechanic, business and laborer would benefit by weekly expenditure of so large a sum. More money in circulation and times would be better. Every successful industry is an attraction for other industries to locate here . . ."

A newspaper report listed the stockholders of Webb

Tile Company as: Blaisdell Bros. (who were also principals in the window glass factory in north Coudersport and before that established a kindling wood factory in Austin), J.M. Carpenter (President), John F. Stone (Secretary), Newton J. Peck, Luther B. Seibert, F.L. Andrews (Director), Frank A. Raymond (Treasurer), H.H. Cobb, Leon E. Larrabee, W.I. Lewis, H. Fitzroy Webb (general manager and superintendent) and Joseph Webb." The article further stated that the company was capitalized at $250,000 to develop the 170-acre property in east Coudersport, an area now referred to as Center Park.

Financing consisted of a $50,000 first mortgage gold bond, issued through the Exchange National Bank of Olean, New York, by the Webb Patent Tile Company.

The valley was abuzz with activity throughout 1900. The Webb brothers forecasted that their plant would produce 15,000 feet of tile per week, as well as plain and fancy glassware, beginning in September.

The factory itself was being built on five acres. An adjacent section was reserved for possible expansion of the Webb plant, or location of separate industries. Dozens of residential building lots were established, with a price tag of $200 each, and construction of new homes began immediately.

A *Potter Enterprise* reporter visiting the site noted that Karl Zimmerman, original owner of the land, had two brick homes built on property he had reserved, using materials produced by his own kiln. The homes are still standing today. Zimmerman would later team with partners George Clark and L.F. Andrews to open a new brickmaking

plant that supplied material for many Coud-ersport area homes and businesses built during the early part of the century.

A crew of 15 men, under the direction of T. J. Keneally, began digging a trench for the gas line in the valley, while another crew working under Fred Andrews dug away at a deep ditch that extended over Benson's Hill, south of the factory site. The closest gas line terminus was six miles away as the crow flew, but a much greater distance in reality because of the rolling hills.

Lute Seibert put his money where his mouth was. By early July, his construction crew had begun work on a three-story, 60-room hotel and boarding house that would become known as the "Dreamy Land Inn." However, for the first couple of years, it was simply called the Seibert Hotel. Seibert, with visions of a swelling population and growing prosperity, sought to make his building a showplace, and he spared no expense. Buildings from the old fairgrounds were razed and, in their place, he erected a Queen Anne-style hotel, complete with an ornamental roofline and other decorations.

While construction of the factory continued, the promoters weren't shy about boosting their product. They claimed the Webb company was the only one in the nation that could produce tile of any color, even matching specific samples that were provided, if the customer so chose. Quality of the product would also vary, depending on size and thickness.

One New York City businessman was said to be interested in buying vast quantities of the

Dreamy Land Inn, built by Lute Seibert in hopes of housing workers from the plant.

A five-hundred dollar bond certificate issued by the Exchange National Bank of Olean, New York, at six percent interest. This is one of the hundred issued to cover the first mortgage on the Webb Patent Tile Company.

tile to cover the walls of a viaduct for a "sub-railway." That order alone was forecasted to keep the plant in operation for five years.

Fire was started in one of the furnaces in early August 1900. On September 12, H. Fitzroy Webb said that both departments would begin to make samples within a week. He predicted the production of 15,000 feet of tile per week in the early stages, and 30,000 feet weekly by mid-October. Neither goal was met.

One of the most important commodities at the Webb plant was water. Not only was water needed for fire protection—fire was the most serious threat to any glass plant constructed during that era—a steady supply was also necessary to assist in the production of glass. Drought sometimes reduced the flow of Mill Creek to a trickle. Work on two large reservoirs—a 38' by 54' pond near the former site of the Zimmerman farmhouse and another reservoir on a hilltop adjacent to the Webb plant—was continuing as late as mid-October, while arrangements were made to tap into the eastern terminus of Coudersport Borough's municipal water system.

Skilled workers were required for many aspects of

The three tiles in the middle and the one at the bottom are completed. The other two items are shards which came from the site. Note the thickness of the smallest shard. This is apparently the blown glass that was fused to the porous backing.

the glass production, and the Webbs recruited dozens of them from the Pittsburgh area. "Quite a number of strangers on our streets," wrote a *Potter Enterprise* scribe. "We are told they are glass blowers for the new plant on East Second Street." The *Enterprise* noted that "four of Ladona's young ladies work in the glass dish factory" ("Ladona" is still the common name for the former village of Lymansville, located just east of the glass plant).

An exact date for the first production is unknown. The October 17, 1900 *Potter Enterprise* reported, "Things are moving along nicely at the Webb Patent Tile Works and for the past 10 days some very handsome (tile) samples have been blown. Mr. Fitzroy Webb, after whom the plant was named, is a very busy man and informed us that by Monday next week the works would be running full-handed and turning out tile for the market. The samples already are very handsome and clearly demonstrate that Mr. Fitzroy Webb is 'master of the situation' in the line of colored glass making. The decorative glassware department, which by the way is sort of a side line, will add much to the life of the Tile Works. Surely East Coudersport is already showing the effects of this great industry. Many new dwellings are already occupied. Many more are near completion. The large hotel is nearly finished. New streets, sewers, water and gas mains are now being laid. This section will before many months equal or rival North Coudersport."

A week later, the newspaper reported that the boarding house was "assuming a prepentious appearance; five houses are in different stages of completion (and the) foundation for another house is nearly completed . . . finishing touches are being put on the H. H. Cobb house; exterior of Gridley house will soon be completed."

The November 7 edition of the *Potter Enterprise* described a distinct "pea vine," or "endless vine," or "bind-weed" pattern that adorned some of the dishware, and noted that decorative dishes were being turned out rapidly. This was the first record of actual production of this unique aspect of "Coudersport Glass." The article made reference to plans for use of the endless vine pattern on spooners, berry dishes, sugar dishes, vases and creamers.

The reputation of Coudersport Glass spread quickly. The Nov. 9 edition of *Commoner & Glassworker* reported, "that portion of the plant occupied by the Joseph Webb Decorative Glass Works is in successful operation."

Meanwhile, the patent for H. Fitzroy Webb's tile that had been so highly praised was met with scrutiny by the courts.

Tragedy nearly struck the factory on the evening of Nov. 28, 1900. Employee C. Beasley went to a small structure where the regulators for the tile plant were kept, intending to set the temperature for the night. As he opened the door, an explosion rocked the facility, likely the result of escaping natural gas being ignited by Beasley's lantern.

Fire burst through the doorway, igniting Beasley's clothing. The victim rolled on the ground in the snow to extinguish the flames and received burn wounds to his face and hands. The fire did not reach the adjacent buildings or cause any appreciative damage to the regulator house.

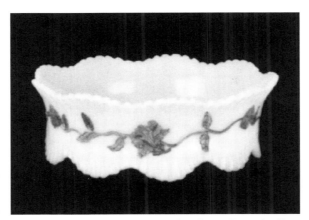

Decorative dishes in the "pea vine," "endless vine" or "bindweed" pattern were being turned out rapidly.

Another accident victim wasn't so fortunate. W. H. Ainsley, son-in-law of Webb Board of Directors President John M. Carpenter, a businessman from nearby Galeton, Pa., had taken a job in the Engine Room. His demise at about 8:00 on the morning of January 30, 1901, was witnessed by George Sutton, a furnace hand, who provided the following account to a newspaper reporter:

"I went down to the engine room to tell Mr. Ainsley to shut off a certain machine, and while there has asked me to help him put a belt on the air pump. He got up on a ladder and I went to the pump to steady the belt on the wheel. The belt was tight and kept slipping off the wheel onto the right side of the shaft, and Mr. Ainsley said in a laughing way, 'Have patience, we will get it yet.' The next time, the belt slipped off on the left side, and off from the wheel of the air pump. As it did so, it whipped over towards Mr. Ainsley and began to wind up on the pulley. Mr. Ainsley saw his danger and began to come down the ladder. Just as he was going to place his foot on a rung, the belt caught his foot and drew him into the shaft. At that minute, he called to me, 'For God's sake, stop it!' I don't know anything about the engines, and didn't know how to stop it. I ran out of the room and called two other men, who stopped the engine, after Mr. Ainsley had gone around the shaft several times, his head striking two large beams at each side of the shaft every time he went around. When the engine stopped, Mr. Ainsley fell to the floor. I think he was killed the first time his head struck."

No one knows how much glass tile was actually produced at the plant, and the extent to which it was sold commercially. The New York City subway contract never materialized. At least a portion of this glass-coated ceramic tile ended up as facing on fireplaces in Coudersport homes. It is possible that the tile works never progressed

beyond the experimental stages, due to the litigation.

Joseph Webb and his group stepped up production of the ornamental glass in time for the 1900 Christmas shopping season. The "Joseph Webb Glassworks" products were on display at the Second Ward Drug Store in Coudersport, described in an advertisement as "handsome vases, dishes; they are beautiful and would make acceptable Christmas gifts."

Additional workers were called in after the holidays from Cleveland, where the glass factory at which they were employed had closed. A newspaper article on January 9 listed them as: B. H. Delahunt, Harry Ashburn, Herbert Pearson, Albert Felter, William Sullivan, Charles Schlermetzauer, Henry Schlermetzauer, Harvey Dunn, Frank Tearney, Charles Felker, Edward Butler Sr., Paul Desmond, Eugene Lang, Victor Lang and William Dyer. Within a week, five of them had relocated to another glass factory in Hazelhurst, Pennsylvania, 50 miles west of Coudersport.

Most of the people employed in the glassmaking profession were itinerants. For example, J.C. Beitler, a skilled painter who had supervised the Decorating Room in the ornamental glass portion of the Webb plant, had painted designs on bathtubs and produced oil and water color works before he arrived in Coudersport.

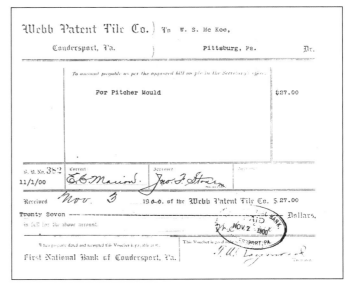

Webb Patent Tile Co. voucher for a pitcher mold, payable at First National Bank of Coudersport; paid on Nov. 7, 1900.

15

Some of the items donated to the Potter County Historical Society by Marcia Beitler Newitt.

Beitler's daughter, Marcia Beitler Newitt, was born in Coudersport in 1901. Her family moved to Chicago in 1903, where her father was employed in a china factory before striking out on his own, painting china and giving art lessons. Beitler went on to become a catalog illustrator for merchandising giants Sears, Roebuck & Company and Montgomery Ward. Later, he painted church murals and decorated glass for church windows.

From there, Beitler moved on to other ventures, including lampshade painting and polychroming metal-framed furniture. He was working for a lamp company as a decorator at the time of his accidental death in 1933. As a tribute to her father, Marcia Beitler Newitt donated eleven samples of the higher-quality Coudersport Glass that remained in her family to the Potter County Historical Society Museum.

Frances Kelly Beckman, whose parents owned a bakery in downtown Coudersport, recalled stories her parents, William and Rose Kelly, told of the colorful characters who worked at the plant and boarded with her family. These fun-loving workers enjoyed their leisure time, spending much of it at Kelly's Bakery. Frances and her younger brother Blake would dance on the display cases to entertain them. Frances recalled her family telling of the Christmas Eve when her grandmother prepared a large pot of oyster stew for the workers who could not go home for the holidays.

Low gas pressure in early January 1901 forced workers to supplement the fuel supply with wood, keeping some of the furnaces burning. Others were shut down and pro-

duction was interrupted in a portion of the plant.

Once the Webb Patent Tile Company and Joseph Webb Decorative Glass Works were a established, labor union leaders moved in. Local Union No. 76 of the American Flint Glass Workers' Union was organized in Coudersport during the first week of February 1901.

Not long afterward, the Webb plant suffered a critical blow: H. Fitzroy Webb was told by the court that his patent was encroaching on another. He was forced to halt the production of tile, shifting the entire focus of the factory to Joseph Webb's decorative glass.

This created some unrest and bitterness within the community, particularly among the stockholders. This story in the April 11, 1901, *Potter Enterprise*, printed under the headline, "Changed To Glass Factory—Tilemaking A Failure," provides some indication:

"Several weeks ago rumors were afloat to the effect that the necessary alterations would be made to change the Webb Patent Tile Company's factory into a window glass factory, and present indications are that such alterations will soon be made, as it is said that the stockholders are of the opinion that this is the only possible way in which they can hope to get interest on the money they have invested. However, nothing definite has been made public. While the manufacture of fancy glassware as carried on by this factory is an expensive process, so much so that the completed goods cannot be sold at as low figures as those manufactured in factories of a similar nature, changes here may also be made which will enable the stockholders to run this department on a paying basis. The manufacture of glass tile has resulted in a complete failure and no further efforts will be made to manufacture the tile. To the outsider, it would seem that the capitalists of Coudersport have learned a severe, costly lesson which should make them more guarded in their future investments."

The owners redoubled their efforts to make the ornamental glassmaking a success. The Webbs signed on with a well-connected manufacturers' representative, Frank M.

Above: Barbershop Quartet, circa 1901–1902, made up of workers from the Coudersport glass plants.

Right: Kelly Bakery and Restaurant, Main Street, Coudersport, Pennsylvannia. This photo is also from the 1901–1904 period. The building still stands and was occupied by Susie Q's Dress Shop until just recently. The owners, Rose Kelly (in front) and William Kelly (third from left), are shown with some of the glassworkers. These men spent a lot of their leisure time at the restaurant, enjoying the Kelly hospitality.

Left: A group of workers from Coudersport glass plants, enjoying themselves (note the members of the quartet in this photo).

The photographs and information on this page were supplied by Roseanne (Beckman) Weidman, Rehoboth Beach, DE; Roberta (Beckman) Pioli, Rockville, MD; and John Beckman, Coudersport, PA, grandchildren of Rose and William Kelly.

17

Miller of New York City, to seek wider distribution of Coudersport Glass. The leading attraction for the upscale market was Webb's own "Pompeii Ware," available in a variety of shapes with a greenish-gold iridescent effect.

On the other hand, the "bindweed" or "endless vine" pattern was produced cheaply and in large numbers, and could be purchased by anyone for a few cents.

Fortunately for historians, a reporter for the *Potter County Journal* visited the Coudersport Glass factory in late April 1901 and provided a detailed account of his observations. It is possible that the owners, seeking to generate some 1901-style "spin," enlisted the *Journal's* cooperation:

"Coudersport during the past decade has undergone a great transformation. To give the *Journal* readers a true conception of its expansion in population, educational, and religious advantages, commercial and transportation facilities and manufacturing enterprises would require a modest volume. Among the agencies that have contributed to the material wealth, to the enlightenment and culture of its citizens, and to its prominence in the realm of new enterprises, the *Potter County Journal* can claim an honorable position as it advocates every movement that enhances the town's welfare and prominence.

"With these reflections in mind and prompted by the spirit for news, a representative of this paper wended his steps in an industrial institution in the eastern portion of the town, Coudersport's Glass Tile Works. Upon arrival at the glass plant, the reporter was promptly taken in charge by H. H. Cobb, one of our enterprising businessmen. In his usual genial manner he escorted the reporter to the sample room. Here is an array of decorated vases, spice holders, pitchers, butter dishes, lamp shades, paperweights, fruit and cake trays in all degrees of exquisite styles, colors, hues, tints and shades tastefully and securely arranged.

"While feasting on this beautiful exhibition, W. T. Dike, the affable and proficient book and timekeeper, came to the aid of the scribe. When questioned as to the prospects of the plant, it was said that orders were on hand which will keep the factory on full-time until the first of July. Shipments are made daily, a large one on Tuesday. 1,300 gross of sundry articles are now being made for one firm in Chicago. 3,500 gross of jelly tumblers for another firm and several large orders from the Pan-American Management are at hand. The above-named articles designed for the cottage as well as the mansion will undoubtedly be introduced into prominent markets and sold at a price not exorbitant to the purchaser, yet adequate to return to the investor a fair return for his capital.

"In the decorating room, Mr. J. C. Beitler has the supervision. Here we found G. H. Hughes, a former basket maker, and Miss Anna Knechtel exercising their artistic taste, skill and industry, embellishing the various dishes and other useful commodities, and well do they perform their ornamental duties. From here we proceeded to the furnace and blowing department under the guiding and molding influence of Mr. G. E. Elden, an efficient and experienced gentleman. Every detail comes under his discerning eyes. It is a pleasure to witness the dextrous manipulations of the various mechanisms by the men and boys so earnestly engaged. The writer was informed that one of the blowers during the period of nine hours molds 1,400 paperweights. One of the most skillful employees here is Joseph Wenzel.

"But the cunning hand can only execute that which the mind apperceives and recombines. First the idea, then the symbol, is an axiomatic principle; this is recognized in all industrial achievements. Therefore the next objective point was the designing, model and foundry department. Here we found the inspiring genius and directing power to be William Terlinde and as might be expected, a robust, well-trained German, a master in the art, and associated with him are a half-dozen or more faithful and competent assistants. Models are drawn on paper, molded in lead, carved from wood and engraved into iron, and at different stages of completion were shown. It is surprising what beauty to perfection can be delineated by the human mind. The graceful line symmetric form leafy vines and waving banners, in harmonious simplicity yet blended design, are here imbedded into the woods and metal patterns. All of the molds are designed and made ready for use in this room.

"Space will not permit extended comments about other interesting features and activities—the large substantial buildings, transportation facilities, up to date appliances, securing of supplies and the clock-like superintendence, monthly payroll and accounting system. The nicely-running machinery guided by a trusted expert engineer; the ovens, furnaces, the packing of the goods, and the crushing of rocks; the surrounding landscape and value of this establishment to the town; would no doubt make instructive reading. The courteous bearing of the gentlemanly and lady-like employees are supervising principles, the earnest attention given to their respective responsibilities impress one that the Joseph Webb Glass Works is in the hands of a firm and skilled laborers, who will yet make it a commercial and financial success; make its name a household word and manufacture comforts for those in humble circumstances and luxuries for those possessing wealth."

An artist's rendering of the
Webb Patent Glass Tile Company's
plant in Coudersport, Pa., circa 1900.

The author's exuberance may not have been misplaced when it came to his assessment of Joseph Wenzel, described as a "grinder" in company records. With Joseph Webb's blessings, Wenzel had dabbled in the production of cut glass during his spare time at the plant and was attracting some attention. "He has produced specimens of cut glass dishes that are equal to those manufactured by many of the largest concerns," the *Potter Enterprise* reported on July 1. "The dishes are made after his own pattern and under the closest inspection do not show an imperfection of any kind; so well is the glass cut that experts have been unable to discern a difference when placed with articles manufactured at the famous Hawkes establishment. Mr. Wenzel learned the art of glass cutting at the Hawkes factory, and completed his education in that line at Dorflinger's factory (in White Mills, Pennsylvania). Several . . . have advised Mr. Wenzel to send specimens of his work to leading dealers, confident that he will find a ready market for all that he can produce. If Mr. Wenzel meets with the success anticipated, it is quite probable a company will be formed, more machinery purchased, and the manufacture of the glassware carried on extensively."

That may have been the only ray of hope at the Webb plant. Orders for a large volume of paperweights from the Pan-American Management for its exposition in Buffalo, New York, were hardly enough to keep the fires burning. These clear, rectangular glass blocks with photographic scenes such as churches, waterfalls and area landmarks could be more easily and less expensively manufactured.

Production ground to a halt at the Webb Patent Tile Factory/Joseph Webb Decorative Glass Works in May or June of 1901. H. Fitzroy Webb and Joseph Webb left Coudersport, never to return.

Joseph Webb landed in Sisterville, West Virginia, where he sought the backing of the local Board of Trade for establishment of a 12-pot pressed and blown ware glass factory, to be known as the Tyler County Glass Company. Webb needed $25,000 to start the plant, where fancy dishes and electric globes would be manufactured.

The idea never did catch on. However, Webb did find support in New Martinsville, West Virginia, where a new glass manufacturing plant had opened in May 1901, producing tableware, lamps, novelties and packers' goods. Joseph Webb was named superintendent and, during a three-year stay at the New Martinsville Glass Manufacturing Company, made a name for himself for the production of a Muranese line that some compared to Tiffany glass. Available in water sets, finger bowls, berry sets, vases, electric globes and perhaps other items, this glass featured an outside finish of dead gold, with an inside of burnished gold. The new Martinsville plant produced the glass until March 1907.

After a short stay with the Haskins Glass Company in Martins Ferry, Ohio, Webb was named manager of the struggling Byesville Glass Company (formerly American Art Glass Company) near Cambridge, Ohio. He died on December 29, 1905, at the age of 52 of a protracted illness stemming from malarial fever.

If some Coudersport people felt bitterness toward the Webb brothers because of the tile and glass plant's failure, their viewpoints did not make it into print. The Jan. 4, 1906 edition of the *Wetzel (*W.Va.*) Republican* reported Joseph Webb's death on the front page with this personal portrait: "Mr. Webb was a very pleasant gentleman, one who had traveled extensively, read much and was an entertaining and versatile talker, and a man who by his gentlemanly and kindly manner made many warm friends."

An obituary in *China, Glass and Lamps* called him "a glass maker without peer and an artist in original designing."

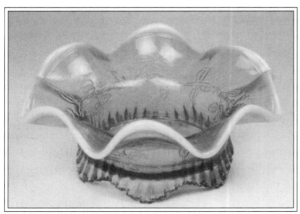

Bastow Glass Co.
1903-1904

Many of the skilled workers from the Webb plant in Coudersport took jobs with other glass plants. Some of the common laborers landed with the new Palmer Window Glass Factory about 20 miles north of Coudersport in Shinglehouse, Pennsylvania (Palmer, which grew to employ 300 people, wisely acquired its own gas leases to save on fuel expenses). Other laborers drifted to another major employer, the Bayless Pulp and Paper Company, 15 miles away in Austin, Pennsylvania.

William Terlinde and a handful of others stayed at the plant, or at least in the vicinity. Terlinde was working on a new glass-blowing machine he eventually patented for the production of milk and fruit jars.

Investors in the Webb plant did not want to be left holding the bag, so they devoted their energies toward reopening the factory, as reported in the August 8, 1901 *Potter Enterprise*:

"The *Enterprise* has been informed by a prominent man, and one of the largest stockholders in the Webb Patent Tile Company's plant, that that industry will very soon be put into active operation, with the object in view of making the capital invested earn a fair rate of interest, which it appears can be done. It is proposed to manufacture glass tile and fancy glassware. The people of Coudersport will welcome this bit of news, as many have held the opinion that the factory would not be operated for some time, and perhaps would remain in its present condition. This opinion is not well founded, as too much money is invested to allow the factory to remain permanently closed."

By the time more specific plans were revealed in late September, the company had been restructured under the name Ladona Glass Company, named for the unincorporated village on the eastern border of Coudersport, just east of the factory. A flattening oven had been removed from the premises and the operators envisioned a new line of products, including fruit jars, bottles and wide-mouthed ware manufactured on Terlinde's machine, as well as skylight glass.

Apparently, some milk jars were manufactured during this incarnation of the plant, but production was lim-

ited and ground to a halt sometime in early 1902, after which the factory sat idle for many months. The stockholders tried to interest other operators, but had no success. By December 1902, the trustees, seeking to cut their

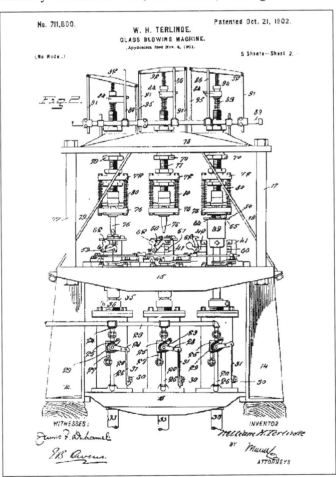

This patented glass blowing machine was comprised of a table having an orifice therein, a sectional mold mounted above the orifice, an ejector sliding under the mold to form the bottom and over the orifice to temporarily close it, and the means for operating the mold sections and ejectors in unison. There was also a method to deliver the molten glass, and many other advanced features. This machine was invented by W.H. Terlinde, an employee of The Webb Decorative Glass Co. Coudersport, Pennsylvania. The patent was approved on October 21, 1902.

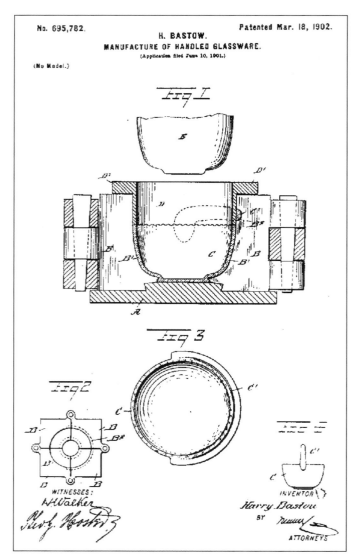

No. 695,782.   Patented Mar. 18, 1902.
H. BASTOW.
MANUFACTURE OF HANDLED GLASSWARE.
(Application filed June 10, 1901.)
(No Model.)

WITNESSES:
A. H. Walker

INVENTOR
Harry Bastow
BY
ATTORNEYS

An application for the patent of this machine was filed by Harry Bastow on June 10, 1901, intended to provide improvements in the manufacture of handled glassware. In this method the handle was cast directly upon the bowl or body to ensure homogeneity between the body and the handle. This rendered the manufacture of the articles less expensive by avoiding the costly process of sticking the handle on the body or bowl after the same is formed separately. It was approved March 18, 1902.

losses, were selling what little they could of the glass which remained stored at the plant.

A plan to reopen the plant for production of window glass in April 1903 was abandoned when Potter Gas Company could not guarantee a supply of natural gas at five cents per thousand feet.

Some of the leftover merchandise found its way to the shelves of Allen's Five and Dime where, in May 1903, customers could buy glass salt and pepper shakers in blue, pink and white—made at the "Ladona Glass Dish Factory"—for a nickel a pair. Glass tumblers ("good quality, smooth edges") were marked down to 30 cents a dozen. A four-piece table set in blue, opal and ivory went for a dime; seven-piece berry sets in opal and ivory were offered at 15 cents.

Three months later, while Allen's was selling 13-inch vases from the defunct Ladona plant for a dime apiece, a noted glassmaker and inventor was plotting to bring the factory back to life. Harry Bastow had started his active connection with the flint glass industry when he became associated with Harry Northwood at Ellwood City, in 1895.

He went on to succeed Northwood in charge of the National Glass Company plant in Indiana, Pennsylvania (still referred to as the "Indiana Glass Company" by residents of the community). Bastow had actively studied chemistry, with special reference to glass, and developed a number of color and decorative effects, as well as patenting certain mechanical improvements.

In August 1900, while the factory in Indiana was closed for repairs, Bastow and others left to establish a competing "fancy glass" factory in Steubenville, named Jefferson Glass Company. Among those traveling with Bastow was Frank Leslie Fenton, a 20-year-old former apprentice who had been a decorating foreman at the Indiana plant in 1898.

Harry Bastow served as president and general manager at Jefferson Glass Company, supervising the production of opaline jugs, tumblers and articles for the ten-cent trade line in various colors while working on his own innovations. These included a process for casting handles directly on the body of glassware, patented by Bastow in May 1902.

Bastow was intelligent, innovative and very knowledgeable of the glass industry, but his arrogance may have caused hard feelings among other company officials. Bastow had also been suffering from a mysterious illness, eventually diagnosed as appendicitis, and was unable to work during the latter part of 1902. It is possible that Bastow was not content to share the limelight, or that he could foresee a vast fortune awaiting him when he could strike out on his own.

For whatever reason, by 1903 he was gone from Steubenville. Bastow arrived in Coudersport to pick up the pieces at the Webb/Ladona plant and resume production of "Coudersport Glass." Traveling with him were Frank L. Fenton and his older brother, John W. Fenton. The Bastow Glass Company signed a one-year lease in early September, with an option to buy the facility.

Bastow and the Fentons had grand aspirations. They would focus on pressed and blown decorated tableware and novelties in a variety of colors. The future for the glass industry in Coudersport looked healthy.

Headlines in the September 10, 1903 *Potter Enterprise* (excerpted below) read:

"Splended New Industry Secured. Webb Tile Plant Leased and to be Running in Few Weeks . . . The old Webb tile plant has been leased to Basto (sic) Glass Company, and it is expected business will begin within six or eight weeks."

Bastow's group joined the Glass Association, a cooperative marketing group, in early October 1903 and devised a plan to produce some eye-catching samples for the Pittsburgh Exposition. Pots, presses and materials were soon acquired. Charles M. Tarr, who accompanied Bastow and the Fenton brothers from Steubenville, was in charge of producing the molds. The plant contained two furnaces and one continuous tank for a total of 28 pots. Harry Bastow, as president of the new company, ensured the investors that he had secured "a pleasing batch of orders."

By late October, glassmaking had resumed at the Coudersport factory, now known officially as The Bastow Glass Company. The plant was advertised as being one of the best equipped in the tableware line. Of particular note was the new operators' decision to continue the traditional Coudersport Glass "bindweed" pattern from the Webb days.

"(Bastow) will make the very finest grades of decorated and colored goods, their purpose being to raise the present standard of these wares considerably," said an article in the November 1903 edition of *China, Glass & Pottery Review*.

The resumption of operations was good news to Lute Seibert, who was doing his best to make his hotel and boarding house—renamed the Dreamy Land Inn in July 1903—the social center in east Coudersport. Visitors were encouraged to stay there for a "secure rest and healthy

Splendid New Industry Secured.

Webb - Tile Plant Leased and to be Running in Few Weeks.

Coudersport is to have a valuable new industry. The old Webb tile plant has been leased to the Basto Glass Company, and it is expected business will begin within six or eight weeks. It looks as if it is a sure go this time as the lease has been made and bonds executed to secure the payment of the obligation involved. The parties interested come from in and about Pittsburg and are experienced in the work.

Decorated dishes, wine sets and other fancy ware, of fine quality will be the principal product of the plant. Some staple work in the line of plain dishes will also be turned out.

It is understood about four hundred persons will be employed when the factory gets well under way, and that two hundred and fifty will be employed from the beginning. Mr. Basto is quoted as saying that he would be able to furnish work to seventy-five girls and as many boys.

Prominent men acquainted with the management of such a plant say this institution will be worth ten times as much to Coudersport as was the glass plant as run by the American Window Glass Company.

It is understood that the campany behind Mr. Basto have the necessary capital to make this a prosperous and growing industry.

A warm welcome certainly awaits all those interested, from all Coudersport.

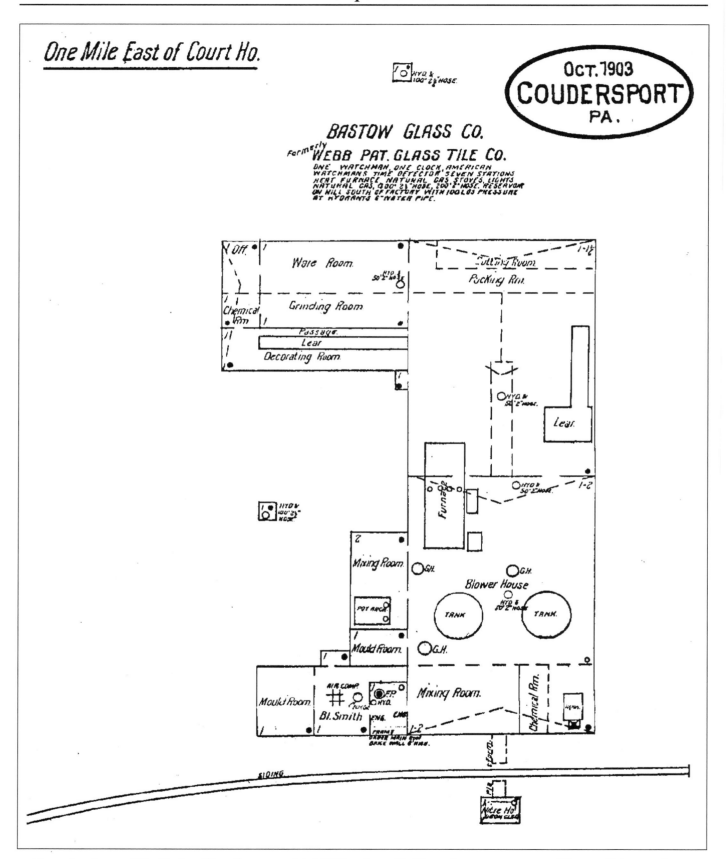

A layout and map of The Bastow Glass Company, dated 1903 and provided by an insurance company. The map lists a watchman, furnace, natural gas stoves and lights, and the location of the reservoir on the hill behind the plant, which is still evident today.

Courtesy of Jim Measell.

climate," and to occupy those rooms that the Webb glass-workers had vacated.

Incorporation papers certified on December 9, 1903, listed Harry Bastow as majority stockholder, while Thomas E. Bastow had a large share, as well. Capital stock totaling $25,000 was offered at $50 a share. As Treasurer, Thomas E. Bastow was paid $2,500 in cash.

There was a large volume of glass produced in late 1903 and early 1904. *China, Glass & Lamps* reported on December 19, 1903, "The Bastow Glass Company at Coudersport, Pa., are making tableware, lantern globes, tumblers, Welsbach shades, card receivers and lemonade sets. They expect to make pressed pitchers, wine sets and novelties in the near future. The nine-pot furnace is being operated and a tank will be started soon."

Bastow placed this ad in the January 1904 *China, Glass & Pottery Review*: "The Bastow Glass Company,

Colored and Decorated Table Ware, Water Sets, etc. Watch for our January Display in Pittsburg."

Locally, the new production from Bastow, and possibly the older pieces from the Webb days, were on hand at Allen's Department Store: "A Grand Special Sale of Glass Dishes at Allen's, made at Coudersport Glass Tile Fac-

This Stock certificate from The Bastow Glass Company was issued to Willis Conable,
great-grandfather of Anona Zwald Green. *Courtesy of Anona and Bob Green.*

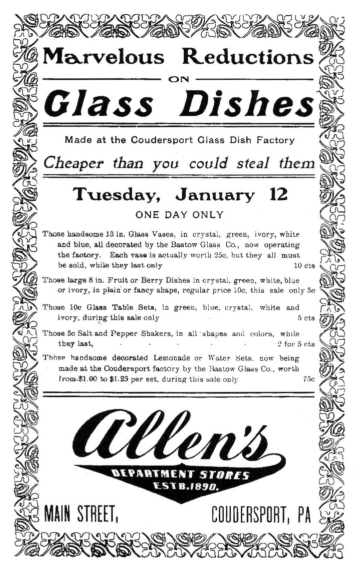

This advertisement for glass dishes on sale at Allen's Department Store appeared in the Jan. 7, 1904 *Potter Enterprise.*

tory and sold at one-half their actual cost. We have just received an enormous stock of these dishes and they are still coming. All kinds, shapes and colors . . . 13-inch vases, fancy or plain tops, in crystal, green, ivory (*Author's Note: this was probably opaque, such as custard glass*), white and blue, all decorated by the Bastow Glass Company, worth 25 cents, for 10 cents; 8-inch fruit and berry dish regularly 10 cents, on sale for 5 cents; glass and table sets in green, blue, crystal, white and ivory, regularly 10 cents, on sale for 5 cents; salt shakers in all shapes and colors, regularly 5 cents, now two and one-half cents; handsome decorated lemonade and water sets, now being made by the Bastow company, a $1.00 to $1.25 value on sale for 75 cents."

Production was apparently slowed in early 1904. *China, Glass & Lamps* reported on February 6: "As soon as the new tank is started, the men at the Bastow Glass Company's works will be enabled to work steadily. A fine line of jugs is being turned out and the company have booked a nice lot of orders for them. The other lines are also going well and they anticipate a steady run up to the end of the season as soon as the tank is in shape."

Even with the slowdown, Coudersport's business community was impressed enough with the Bastow factory to invest in it. In February 1904, after a visit to the plant by a delegation of potential investors, some $5,000 in stock was sold to the following: Potter Gas Company, Richards and Shear, Smith and Dexter, John Clark, M.S. Thompson, G.H. Doane, A.G. Olmsted, A.B. Mann, and Lute Seibert. Stockholders increased the size of the Board of Directors to five, with A.B. Mann and W.H. Richards joining Harry Bastow, Thomas Bastow and W.P. Sweeney.

In March, Harry Bastow was on the road to solicit new orders for his factory. Word soon came from Pittsburgh that Bastow had secured an order for thousands of "lamps," presumably shades and chimneys for gas lanterns. An intriguing entry in a *Potter Enterprise* article announced, "The Bastow Company will soon secure as a stockholder a well-known capitalist."

None of the area glass factories was thriving in early 1904. In Wellsboro, Pennsylvania, about 45 miles east of Coudersport, a glass plant closed its doors for several weeks in April, citing high costs of raw materials, "coupled with the demoralized condition of the glass markets throughout the country which has continued during the whole blast, and the declining price of glass at a season of the year when prices are usually advancing."

Another sign of possible financial problems can be found in the Potter County tax records of 1904, which reveal that the property occupied by Bastow Glass Company was scheduled to go up for public auction in late May, due to nonpayment of back taxes in the amount of $1,606. It is possible that the arrearage can be traced to the Webb regime rather than Harry Bastow's group, since Bastow Glass Company was occupying the factory under terms of a lease.

Whatever its troubles in the early part of 1904, the Bastow Glass Company seemed to be on the rebound. A weekly journal for buyers noted in its April 23 edition: "Active operations were resumed at the Bastow Glass Works, Coudersport, Pa., the latter part of last week. The company has been materially strengthened, and prospects are good for a prosperous run. President Harry Bastow has several new trade winners which will be placed on

Colored and Decorated
Tableware, Water Sets, Etc.,

Send for Catalogue and Prices

The Bastow Glass Co.
Coudersport, Pa.

Advertisement appearing in the April 16, 1904 issue of *China, Glass and Lamps*.

the market shortly. The plant expects to operate steadily until the end of the blast. The outlook is brighter than at any time during the season."

Frank L. Fenton played a prominent role at the factory as manager of the Decorating Department. He placed this advertisement in the *Potter Enterprise* on May 5, 1904: "Wanted! 25 Girls at the Bastow Glass Company, East Second Street, Coudersport, to learn decorating. Girls can make good wages after a few weeks' experience at piece work and before then they will be paid $3.00 per week. After one months' (sic) experience some girls have made $5.00 and $6.00."

None of those positions was ever filled. On the evening of Sunday, May 8, 1904, fire erupted near one of the furnaces in the cellar of the Bastow Glass Company factory, next to the pot arch, where pots were being heated prior to being placed in the furnace.

A watchman discovered the flames and tried to extinguish them with a hose. Failing that, he alerted nearby residents. An alarm was phoned into Coudersport and volunteer firefighters promptly responded. By the time they arrived, the fire, fanned by a strong southeasterly wind, roared through much of the building.

"The flames had gained such a headway it was impossible to stay their progress," said a report in the *Potter Enterprise*. "In a very short time, only a smoldering heap marked the place where the factory had stood . . . The two large smokestacks, the foundations and stone work of the ovens are all that remains of the once well built and expensive factory."

Property damage was estimated at $80,000; of that amount, the building represented about $60,000 and was

insured for just $11,250.

Bastow Glass Company had no insurance on the machinery and material in the plant. That loss was pegged at $20,000.

"If the factory is rebuilt, the people of Coudersport will have to do it," Harry Bastow told a newspaper reporter. "I am completely strapped, and the work of rebuilding will have to be started at once or we cannot hold

Advertisement from the May 5, 1904 *Potter Enterprise*.

the men."

The *Potter Enterprise*, ever the booster, called upon local capitalists to give glassmaking yet another try in Coudersport:

"By making repairs on these (smokestacks and ovens), another factory, suitable for the Bastow Company, could be erected for about $25,000, but it is hardly probable that that amount can be raised. The loss of the factory is a blow to the financial and social interests of Coudersport. It gave employment to about one hundred people and brought to town desirable residents . . . Residents of Coudersport who have the money to invest should form a stock company and erect another factory. It is considered that the money would be well invested, and the industry would certainly be a valuable one for the town."

Both the *Potter Enterprise* and the *Potter County Journal* suggested that the Bastow Glass Company was on the brink of big things at the time of the fire.

"Much sympathy is expressed for the members of the Bastow Company, the majority of them having had invested every dollar they possessed," read the *Enterprise* article on May 12, 1904. "After weathering through many disheartening financial condi-

tions, the promoters had placed the business on a firm and encouraging basis, and future prospects were very bright."

In the *Journal*: "(Bastow) had built up a large and profitable business, with nearly 100 employees and orders on the books for full operation for six months."

China, Glass and Lamps, in what amounts to an obituary on the Webb/Bastow business, summarized the Bastow period in its May 14, 1904 edition (shown below): "Owing to a shortage of finances and slow trade conditions the new company was handicapped at the start and were only beginning to get matters in shape when the fire occurred. It is not thought the plant will be rebuilt. Decorated tea and water sets and lantern globes were the chief product."

Harry Bastow spent some time in the Pittsburgh area immediately after the fire, and upon his return to Coudersport in June 1904, was still trying to find investors to rebuild the glass factory.

Investors were not willing to take a further chance in the glass industry. In fact, there was bitter-ness among some

of the capitalists, who saw their dreams of fortune go up in smoke. "Rebuild? Not by a damned sight!" said one of the investors, John B. Coulston. "We don't want any more glass factories."

Leaving behind a legal quagmire not solely of his own making, Harry Bastow bid farewell to Coudersport that summer. With creditors quick to file claims in the hopes of receiving at least a fraction of what they were owed by Bastow Glass Company, it was evident that the settlement process would drag on for several months.

The list of personal property of The Bastow Glass Co. after the fire was very short.

Listed as "junk" were a safe, lamp bases (no specified quantity), a lathe, 1000 pounds of mould castings, 13 tons of pot shell,ten pounds of sand, a press, 30 blowpipes and 55 moulds weighing "about 5500 pounds." Items listed with a value were two chucks $10.00, two kettles $4.00, 100 jack brick $10.00, two files $.50, a cabinet $5.00, ten stamps 10¢ , and a cash balance of $.88 at The First National Bank of Coudersport, Pennsylvania.

There were balances due on stock subscriptions of A.A.Wood, George E. Bixby and Arthur Mann of Coudersport, and of two Pittsburgh residents Howard Zacharias and J.E. Biesel.

Listed as assets were bills receivable from companies ranging from Massachusetts and Rhode Island to South Carolina and Alabama. (Assuming these were for completed products, a collector still has a chance of locating Coudersport Glass just about anywhere.) These asset accounts totalled $1060.37.

The debts left were far greater than the assets. There were bills owed to suppliers for machines, belts, lead, packaging supplies, draying, membership fees, telegrams, and advertising as well as the glass making supplies. There was an outstanding bill with the Dreamy Land Inn for $40.00 for board, a gas bill with the Potter Gas Co. for $1156.41, rent due to Webb Patent Tile Co. $850.00 and a listed bill with Emily Bastow of $300.00 for money borrowed.

Outstanding notes were with the First National Bank for two loans totalling $2500, with Collins & Elliott for insurance for $288, two notes with the Potter Gas Company for gas $1371.62, Pennsylvania Glass Sand Co. $115.10 and others totalling over $1,000.

Harry and Thomas Bastow had given their personal endorsements along with certain shares of Potter Gas Co. stock as collateral for the bank notes and one of the larger supplier notes.

By far the longest list of payables due was for wages. The list below includes many family names that are still familiar in and around Coudersport. The original list of wages owed had 55 names on it but many could not prove the amount owed them.

List of labor claims as proven by J. Walter Wells
Assignee of the Bastow Glass Co.

Clarence Page .... $	4.13
Melvin Shaffer	9.00
Nelson Hammond	18.27
H. S. Toombs	12.35
Christ Zimmerman	27.00
Frank Toombs	28.57
Ed Conable	8.00
Joe Massey	21.30
Orlo Patterson	6.50
John W. Fenton	18.00
Frank L. Fenton	69.22
Geo. Keynote	11.85
Neva Elderkin	1.50
Chas. Elderkin	3.00
Lloyd Washbaugh	11.15
A. F. Nelson	63.47
John Bennett	21.30
Geo. Zell	18.00
Harry Bastow	519.00
Joseph E. Bastow	143.00
Frank Berdanier	6.40
H. W. Leygh	23.00
W. Vosburg	30.62
Warren Gridley	48.50
E. L. Fairbanks	27.00
A. M. Snyder	36.75
Lute Westfall	45.00
J. W. Whalen	9.00
Fred Reynolds	29.10
F. Gordnier	8.10
C. M. Tarr	97.90
Thomas Bastow	84.86
Willie Witcomb	4.50
Frank McLaughlin	4.50
R. N. Hammond	7.88
H. Wilson	14.69
Charles Ryan	48.50
Chas. Bly	11.00
Conrad Bly	35.77

Bigger and better things lay ahead for Harry Bastow and the Fenton brothers. Frank L. Fenton moved to Wheeling, West Virginia, to work briefly as a decorator at the H. Northwood Company factory there. Despite the frustrations and setbacks of his early career, Fenton was coming into his own. Within a short time, he realized that he could achieve more. "My particular work was in the matter of design," he said, "and then I got the idea that if I could do this work for an employer, I certainly could do something for myself."

In July 1905, Frank L. and John Fenton rented space in what was the Haskins Glass Company building in Martins Ferry, Ohio, and opened their own decorating shop, the Fenton Art Glass Company. Another brother, Charles H. Fenton, soon joined them. In November 1906, the company relocated to Williamstown, West Virginia, just across the Ohio River from Marietta, Ohio. They built a new plant and began to make glass there on January 2, 1907. The Fenton name is today known throughout the world in association with fine glass products.

Harry Bastow separated from the Fentons after the Coudersport fire, but rejoined the Fentons when they began their company in Martins Ferry. Bastow and John W. Fenton played roles in arranging for the relocation of the Fenton firm from Martins Ferry to Williamstown. Bastow was retained as a consultant to make some of the many arrangements required for such a move.

Relations between Bastow and the Fentons would sour over issues pertaining to the relocation. In November 1906, Bastow sued the Fentons for breach of an oral contract, seeking $15,000 in damages. After a lengthy trial, a jury settled the matter by awarding Bastow a mere $150.

In 1908, Harry Bastow opened the Bastow Manufacturing Company in Weston, West Virginia, producing tableware and lighting goods. This business occupied a large brick building considered to be almost fireproof. It was destroyed by fire in March 1909. The factory was rebuilt and enlarged later that year, and it prospered for a time.

Bastow was with the West Virginia Optical Glass Company in Wheeling as of 1912. He published a book entitled *American Glass Practice* in 1920.

After the fire, the Potter County Circuit Court had frozen the assets of Bastow Glass Company, such as they were. A court-appointed auditor filed a settlement statement on June 23, 1904, but some of the matters were disputed. Funds were not distributed until June 15, 1905. Of the preferred labor claims, Frank L. Fenton was awarded $69.22 and John W. Fenton received $18.

Someone reminded Lute Seibert of his claim that glassmaking would cause Coudersport to become a met-ropolitan area along the lines of Philadelphia or New York. Seibert likened it to the Revelation of St. John the Divine: "It was there on paper, but no one has seen it."

Seibert's Dreamy Land Inn continued to serve meals and host dances, but did not become the social center Seibert had envisioned. It was razed in 1921.

As the years passed, the remains of the Webb/Bastow building were cleared and the property was used as a livestock pasture.

Decades later, laborer Floyd Bliss of Coudersport was installing a drainage ditch at the plant site when he unearthed a pile of glass, including many good-sized pieces in pink, blue, custard, green and lavender in opaque glass; chunks of transparent glass in blue, pink, green, amber and clear; shards of overlay—pink on blue, pink on white, blue on white, and green on white. The only complete piece in the collection was a glass salt cellar, badly heat-warped from the fire.

As fate would have it, Bliss was also an antique collector of no small repute. The farmer on whose land he was working gave Bliss several more fine chunks for his collection. He then began to search for finished glassware made at the plant, which could be authenticated by families who owned the items, or which corresponded with the shards he had found.

Volunteers from the Potter County Historical Society have since actively sought archives from the Coudersport plant and have established a display at the society's museum in downtown Coudersport.

Pieces still show up from time to time at yard sales, flea markets, antique shows and estate sales. Collectors have been frustrated for years by their inability to locate any catalog or substantive advertisement of Coudersport Glass. Adding to the difficulties is the lack of any branding or other manufacturer's mark to verify the origin of most of the pieces. This is typical of many brands produced during the 1902–1904 era; over 95 percent of pressed or blown tableware was not marked.

Therein lies the challenge that has confronted historians and collectors for decades—identifying which pieces came from the Webb or Bastow plants in Coudersport and locating items which are mentioned in newspaper articles or trade journals, but have not surfaced in any known collections of Coudersport Glass.

Coudersport Glass and The Author

Located in the north-central Pennsylvania community of Coudersport, this small glass manufacturing plant produced what would be considered some very elegant and unique items. In the last few years, the number of people forming collections has grown rapidly. Coudersport glassware is being discovered by collectors of Early American pressed glass, as well as milk, custard, vaseline, art glass and a host of others. Prior to this rise in popularity, Coudersport was only collected by a handful of people from this area.

Since 1982 when Bob Currin and I began giving presentations on the subject, we have been repeatedly asked where one can find written information and documented pictures of this beautiful glass. At that time, the only published information available was an article written by Floyd Bliss in the November 1972 edition of *Spinning Wheel* magazine.

As a result of that article, glass researcher and author William Heacock sought out Floyd Bliss to borrow a few of his opalescent pieces for a book entitled *Opalescent Glass From A to Z* (Antique Publications, 1975). "Bill" also included some of Bliss's glassware in his 1976 book *Custard Glass From A to Z*, and was the first person to place a value on Coudersport glass.

It was about this time that I became friends with Bill Heacock. We naturally discussed my growing collection of Coudersport and he often reminded me of the need for a comprehensive book on the subject, suggesting that I take on the project. My response was always "someday when I have time." Soon, the same question was asked of me by so many people that I finally began researching the subject. I had no idea that it would take over ten years to bring this book to completion.

Through our family's involvement with the local newspaper, I was able to print an article eliciting the use of private pieces of Coudersport glass that were not represented in my collection. The generosity of so many people who offered their glass for photography allowed us to show a complete range of manufactured items in the color section of this book (pp. 33–80).

Most of the conclusions in this book are my own. The absence of documentation to authenticate Coudersport patterns has been a challenge. I have conferred with other knowledgeable people on the subject, talked to collectors who have dug shards at the factory site, and combined their opinions with mine. With their help, and based on what limited information I found after many hours of research, I have strived to present a thorough and comprehensive book on the subject.

Even so, I am sure there are discrepancies and missed items. There may even be errors in the list of glass items that I attribute to the Coudersport plant. Maybe publishing this information will help get some of these areas corrected. I look forward to hearing from readers who have constructive ideas on the contents of this book.

As I mentioned earlier, I've received help and support from a large number of people, and hope that I haven't missed giving credit where credit is due. If this is the case, I am truly sorry. I would like this book to record the page in Coudersport history that was previously missing. I hope the historians will be pleased, the collectors of Early American pressed glass will find it useful, and most of all I hope it is enjoyable reading for everyone.

Tulla Majot
RR #1, Box 35
Austin, PA 16720

October 1999

Coudersport Glass in Color

This portion of the book is dedicated to showing Coudersport glass in its own exquisite colors. The variety of shapes, patterns, colors and decorations available is amazing considering the short time that this plant was actually in operation.

For of all sad words of tongue and pen, the saddest are these: 'It might have been!'

As we view these photographs of glassware from the Coudersport factory, we can only dream about what might have been. The scope and beauty of Coudersport glass is impressive. No doubt under different circumstances, this small factory would have gone on to produce a line of wares equal or superior to the other glasshouses that became standards in the industry.

The reader might notice a strong resemblance in shapes and decorations to H. Northwood & Company, Fenton Art Glass and Jefferson Glass among others. The same men that began the Coudersport firm went on to work at these—and other—famous glass factories of this era. Decorators also moved from one plant to another , carrying their techniques with them.

Pages 33 through 63 are arranged chronologically by pattern, with the more typical pressed glass pieces preceding the later items (such as Waffle & Vine, and Three Fingers and Panel). The order is not perfect, but approximate. Pages 64 through 77 show vases, water sets, miscellaneous mold-blown items, and whimseys. Pages 78 through 80 deal with the importance of Stag & Holly, and some reproduction items.

The header on each page describes the pattern or decoration shown, and the number assigned each item is used for identification purposes. These numbers correspond with the description (see pages 81–122) and the value (pages 125–128).

The description for each piece includes its color, pattern, decoration, type of ware and other pertinent facts about the item. Unless otherwise stated, the glass shown is from my own personal collection.

WEBB PATENT TILE

The three tiles in the middle and the one at the bottom of this photo are completed tiles in different shades and sizes. Shown at the top of the photo are two tile shards from the factory site. The thickness of these shards is shown by the smaller shard. This appears to be the blown glass that was fused to the porous backing. The Webb Tile was made in colors ranging from pastels to the darker shades as shown by the fireplace below.

Some of the nicer homes in the Coudersport area feature tiles from the Webb Patent Tile Company in the construction of their fireplaces. This fireplace is in the home of former Senator James Berger, now owned by Carl and Linda Roberts.

PAPERWEIGHT DETAILS

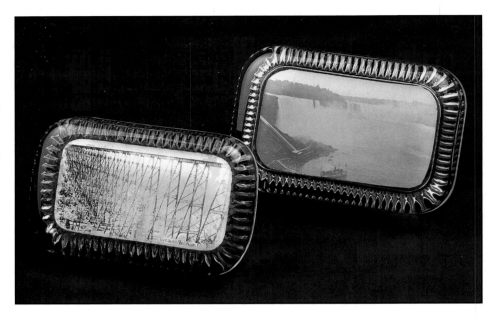

These two paperweights were made from different batches of glass, showing the variations that can be found. Note the different cast to the clear glass.

The Niagara Falls paperweight (*far right*) is 1⁷/₈" x 4¹/₄" x ¹³/₁₆" high. The top is slightly domed. The picture is in sepia tones, framed by a dark backing.

The Kinzua Bridge paperweight (*right*) measures 2¹/₂" x 4¹/₁₆" x ⁵/₈" high. The dome on the top is so minute it appears completely flat. The sepia tones of the picture are starting to fade, possibly due to the fact that the backing (which is a deep green paint) has been partially washed or scratched off. Green paint still remains in most of the grooves, causing the edges of the picture to look somewhat shaggy. The picture covers the entire back of the paperweight, actually touching the base of the grooves.

"ONE GLASSMAKER COULD MAKE 1,400 PAPERWEIGHTS IN A NINE-HOUR DAY."

Coudersport newspaper reporter

These two views of the Pan American Exposition paperweight show the domed effect on the top as well as the thickness. The measurements are 2⁵/₈" x 4¹/₈" x ⁷/₈" high. The picture completely fills the flat area for mounting. The backing is a light piece of paper. The view on the right shows the detail in the buildings, and vivid colors in the sky and foliage.

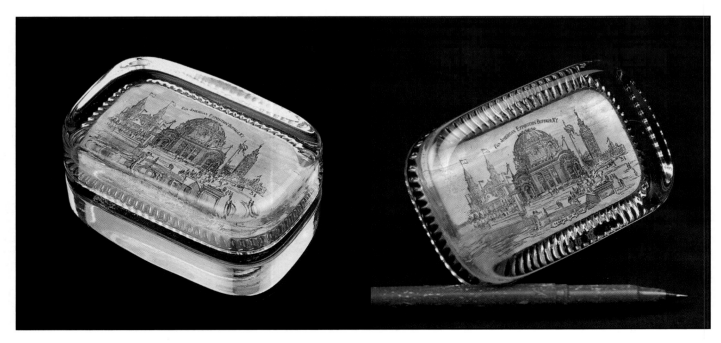

1

2

3

4

5

6

7

8

9

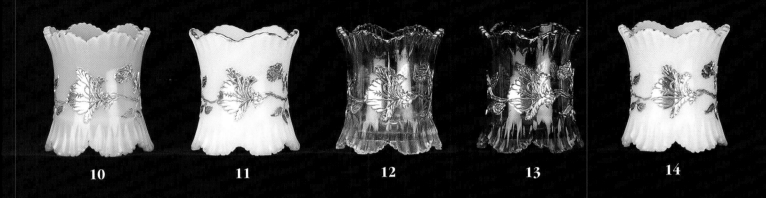

10   11   12   13   14

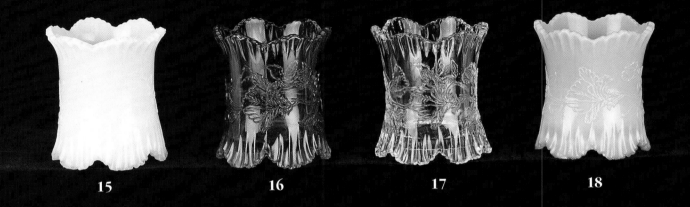

15   16   17   18

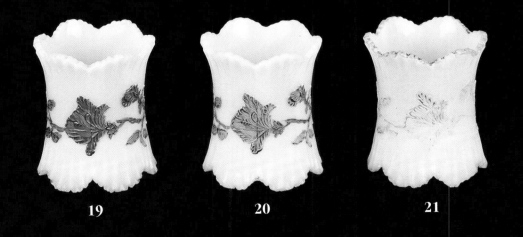

19   20   21

BLUE OPAQUE AND BASKETWEAVE

A complete Berry Set would consist of the master berry bowl and six smaller berries.

Basketweave Condiment Set with an original mustard top.

Ladies' Spittoon made from a Trailing Vine sugar base, believed to be one of a kind.

Trailing Vine, blue opaque

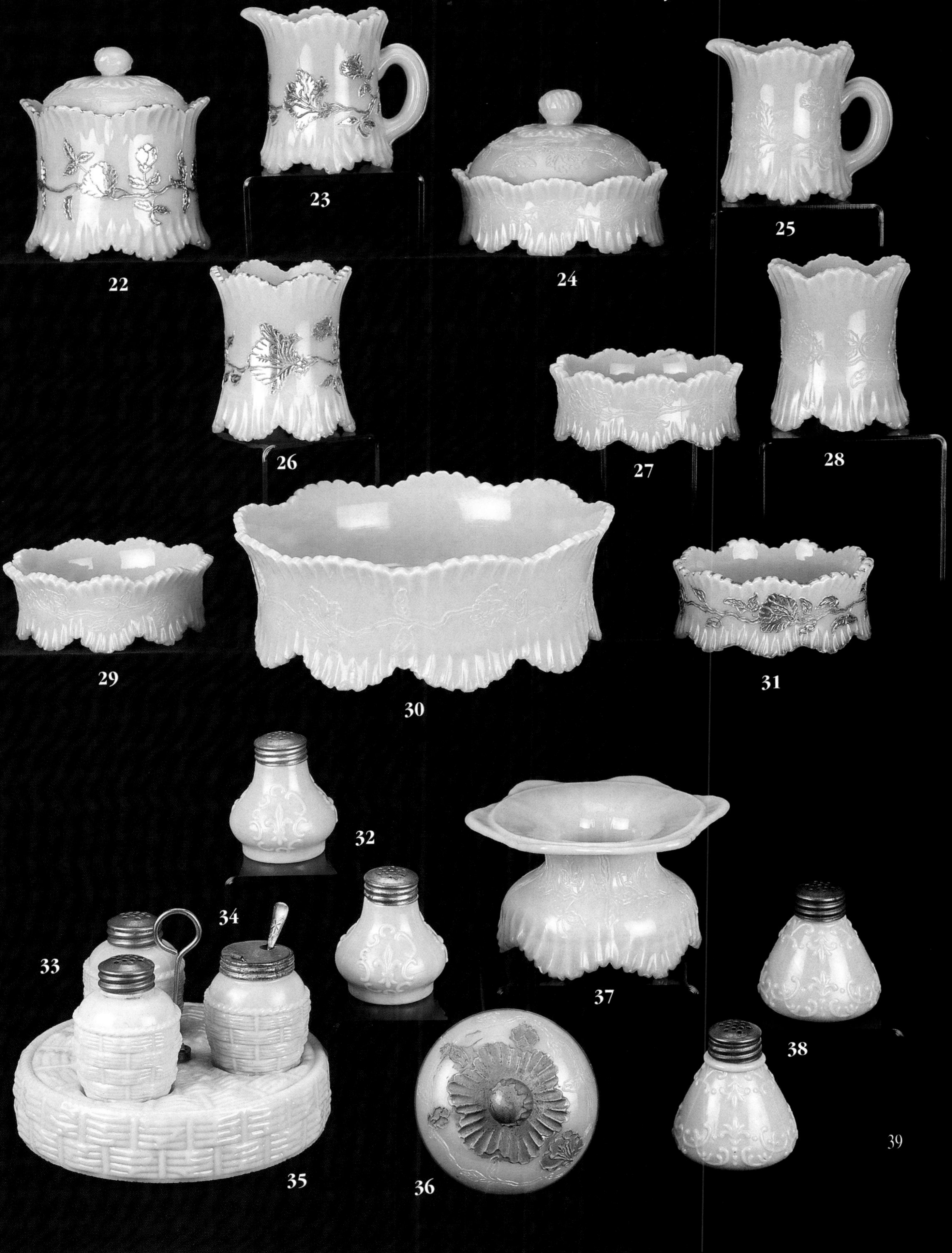
22
23
24
25
26
27
28
29
30
31
32
33
34
35
36
37
38

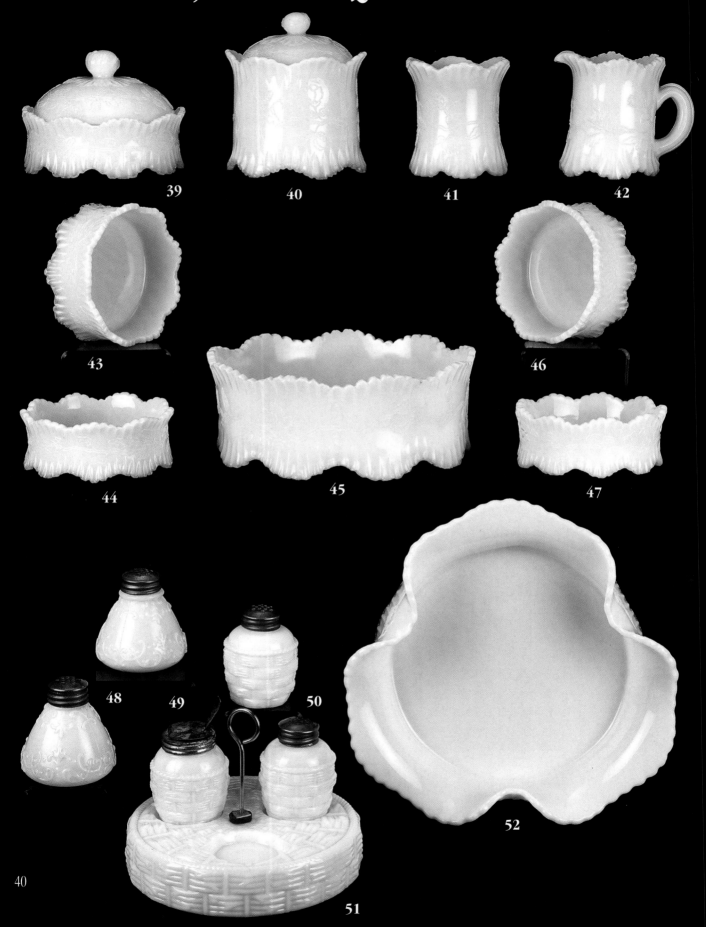

39

40

41

42

43

46

44

45

47

48

49

50

52

51

53

54

55

56

57

58

59

60

61

62

63

64

BASKETWEAVE CONDIMENT SET

65 66 67

TRAILING VINE, GOLD DECORATED

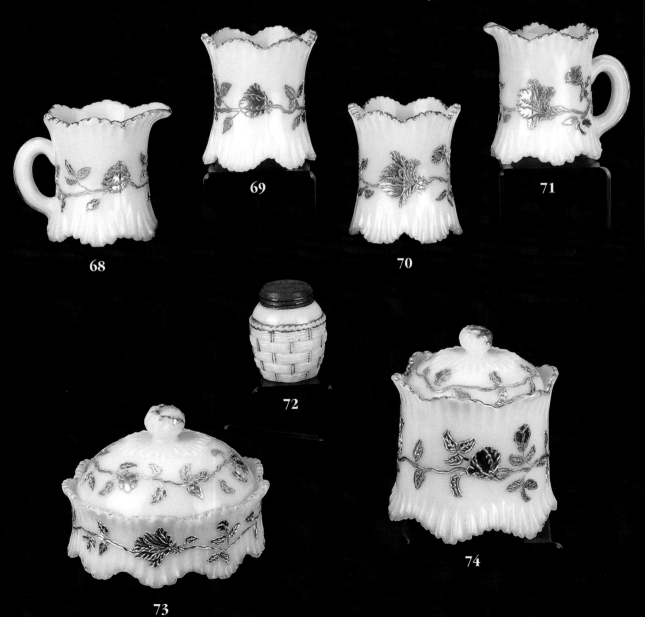

68 69 70 71

72

73 74

42

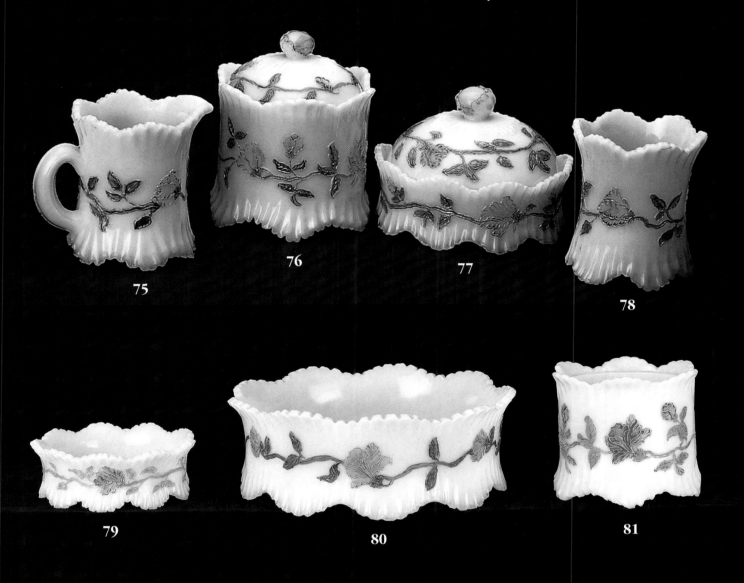

75

76

77

78

79

80

81

82

83

84

85

86

TRAILING VINE, *CUSTARD*

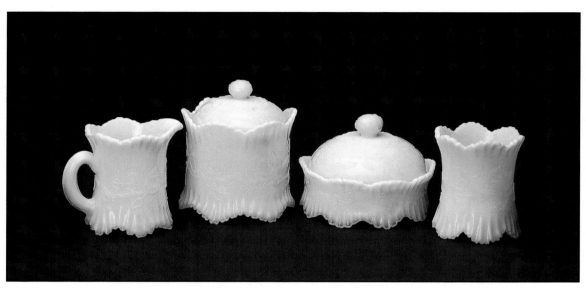

Tableware Set

Master Berry Bowls

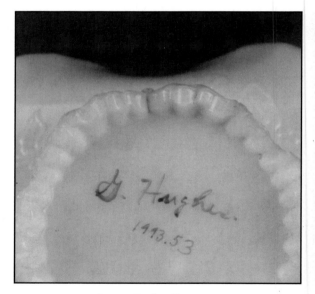

Gomer Hughes Signature

Custard Trailing Vine with gold decoration.

91

92

93

94

95

96

97

98

99

100

101

102

103

45

TRAILING VINE, TRANSPARENT GREEN

Tableware Set with gold decoration.

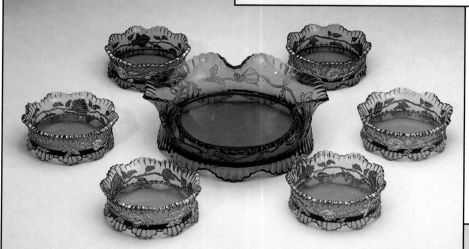

Complete Berry set, consisting of Master Berry and six smaller bowls. The rim of this Master Berry has been drawn inward at three different points. Note the different shades of transparent green within the set.

This photograph shows pattern details. The Trailing Vine encircles the base of the piece, and is repeated on the lid. The leaf effect travels upward onto the finial.

104   105   106

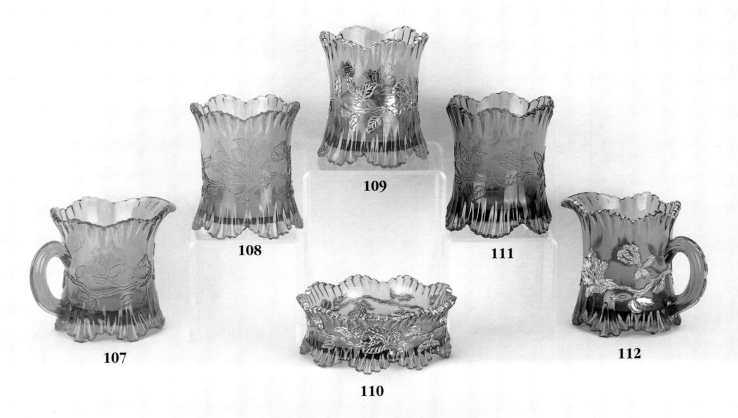

109

108   111

107   112

110

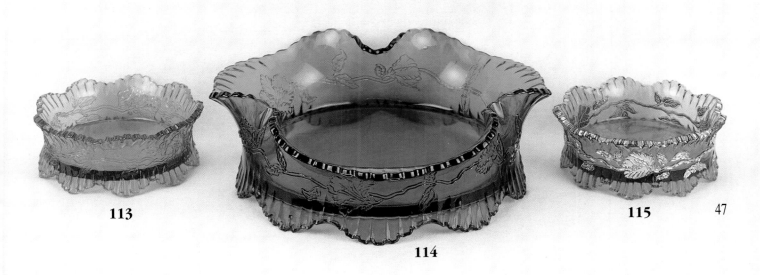

113   115   47

114

TRAILING VINE, RARE

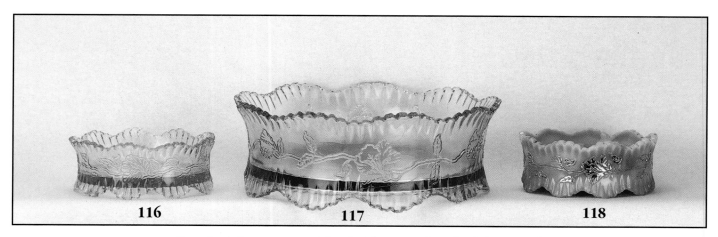

116 **117** **118**

Berry bowls in transparent pink and pink opaque. Considered the rarest of
Coudersport colors, very few pieces were made in pink.

119

This small vase in amber is a very rare piece. The
vase was shaped by drawing the top of a spooner
inward while the glass was still hot. Note the
touch of opalescence on the top edges.

Crystal Trailing Vine in various shades.
In this pattern, very few crystal
items have been located.

48

120

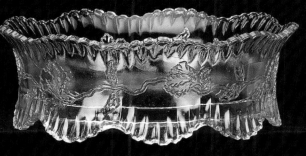

121

122

123

124

125

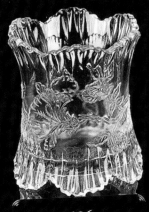

126

127

128

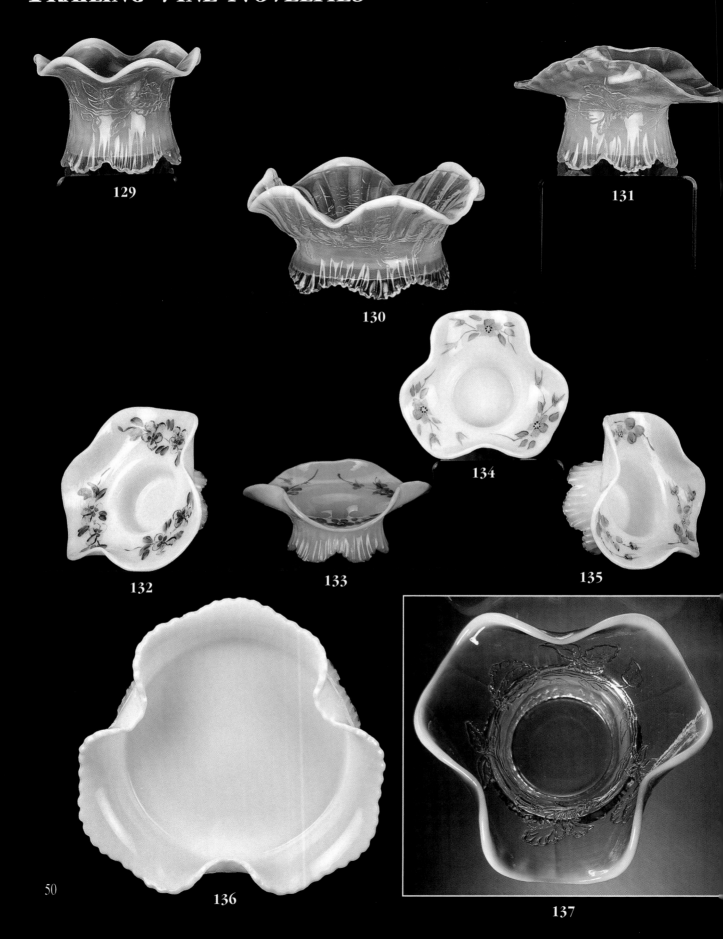

129

130

131

132

133

134

135

136

137

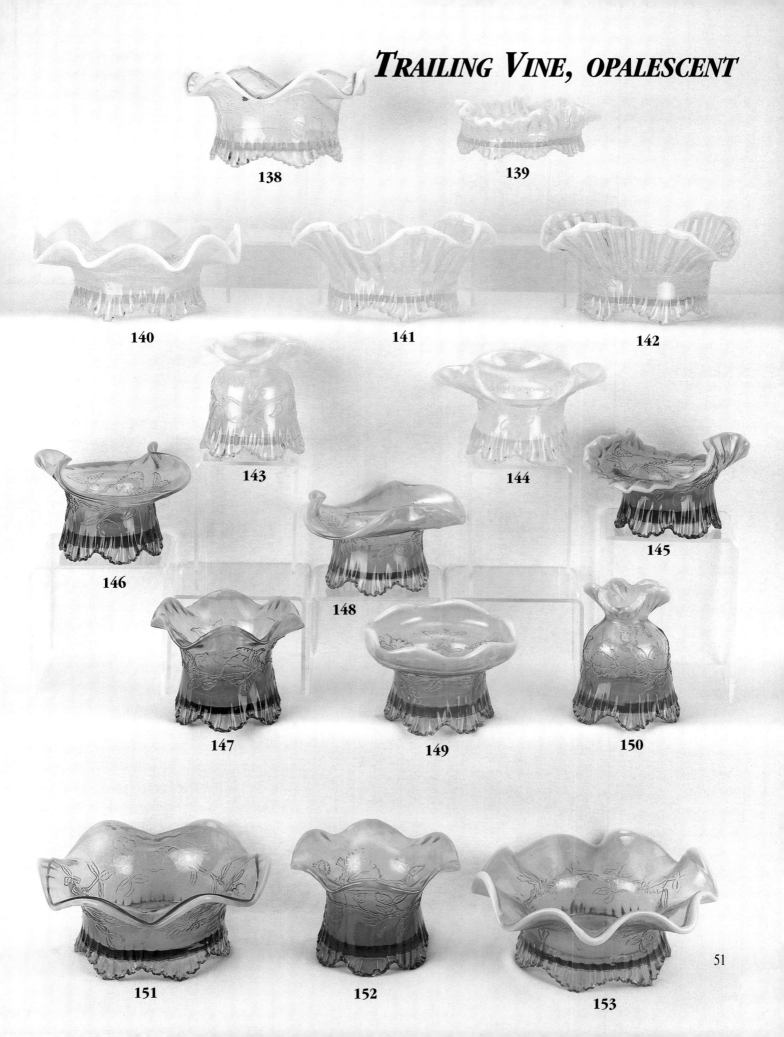

138

139

140

141

142

143

144

145

146

148

147

149

150

151

152

153

51

SHADOW

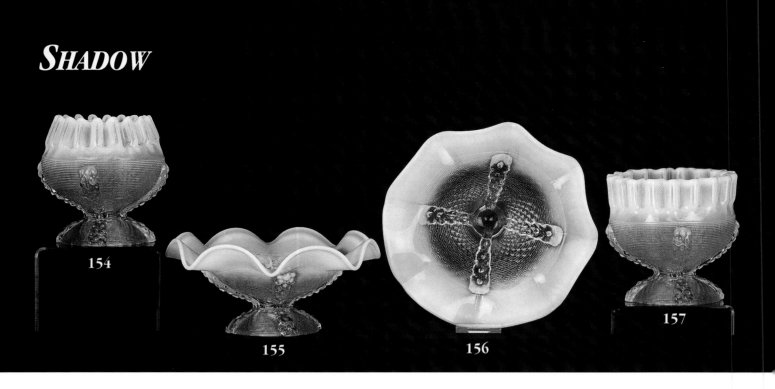

154   155   156   157

Coudersport's Shadow pattern was made in three shapes, all originating from the same footed bowl (or compote) mold.

The Shadow pattern in transparent green. We have not found any evidence to indicate that Coudersport made Shadow in green opalescent.

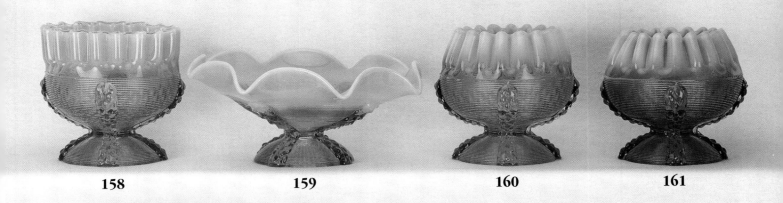

158   159   160   161

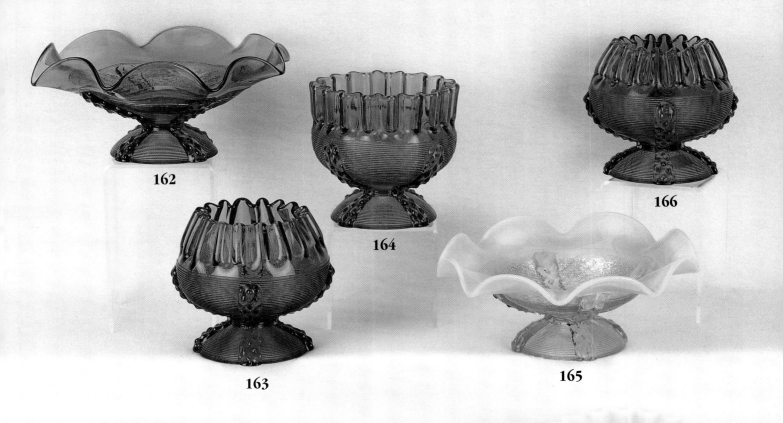

162

164

166

163

165

167   168   169

53

SALT & PEPPER SHAKERS

170 171 172 173

Fantasia shakers in various shades of blue.

Below: Fleur de Lis and Fantasia shakers in opaque white.

174 175 176 177

Below: Pink Fleur de Lis shakers including the one-of-a-kind satin shaker.

Below Right: Rare Basketweave Condiment Set in opaque white.

54

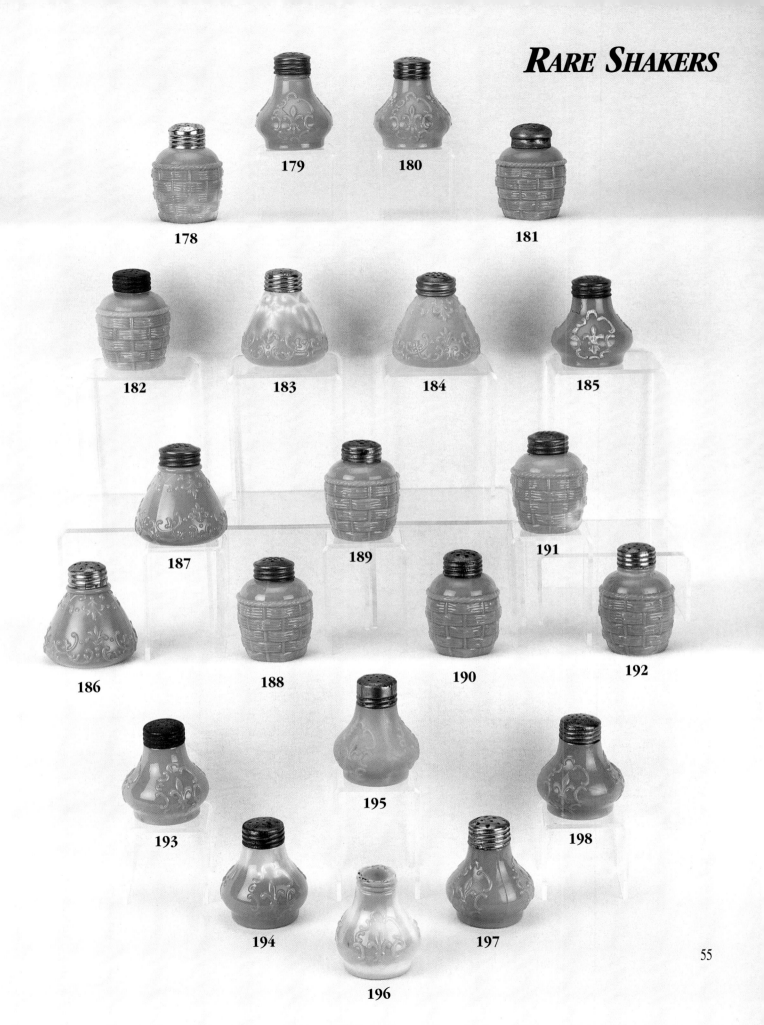

179

180

178

181

182

183

184

185

187

189

191

186

188

190

192

193

195

198

194

197

196

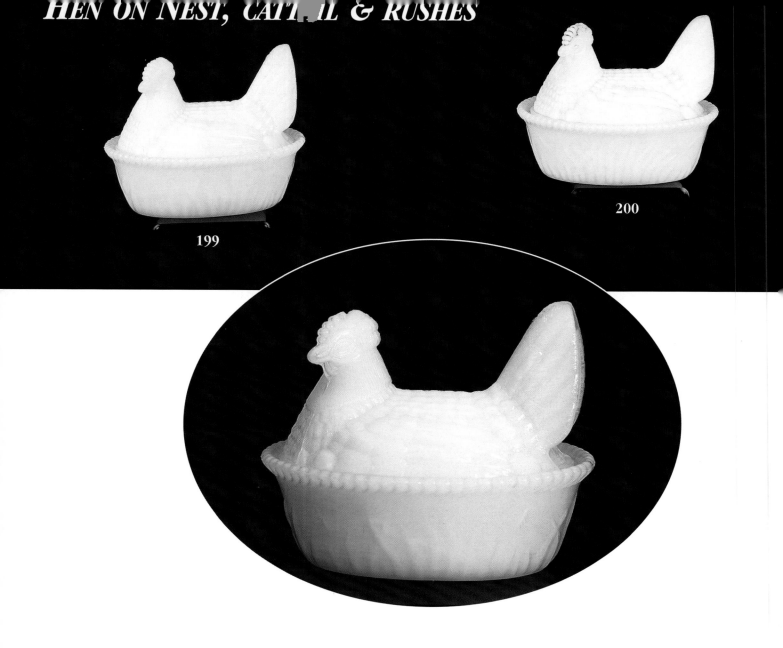

199

200

The nest on the Coudersport Hen covered dish has cattails and rushes reaching towards the rope-style edge. This piece has only been found in white opaque. *(Sketch by Joey Majot)*

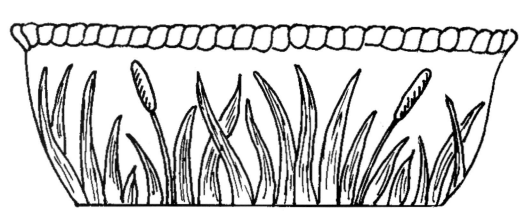

56

201 202 203 204

Three Fingers and Panel was made in white opaque and blue opaque.

These sets were sold to various companies who filled them with condiments for resale. The creamer and sugar were both made with an inner lip to hold the lids securely in place. A cardboard liner rested on the lip, separating the packaged condiment from the lid.

The remains of an old Westmoreland Glass label on a creamer in this pattern is fruit for speculation. It is believed that the Westmoreland Specialty Glass Company (of Grapeville, Pa.) may have copied this pattern, or that the mold may have been moved there before the tragic fire at Coudersport.

205   206   207

208   209

210

WAFFLE & VINE, RARE

211

212

213

214

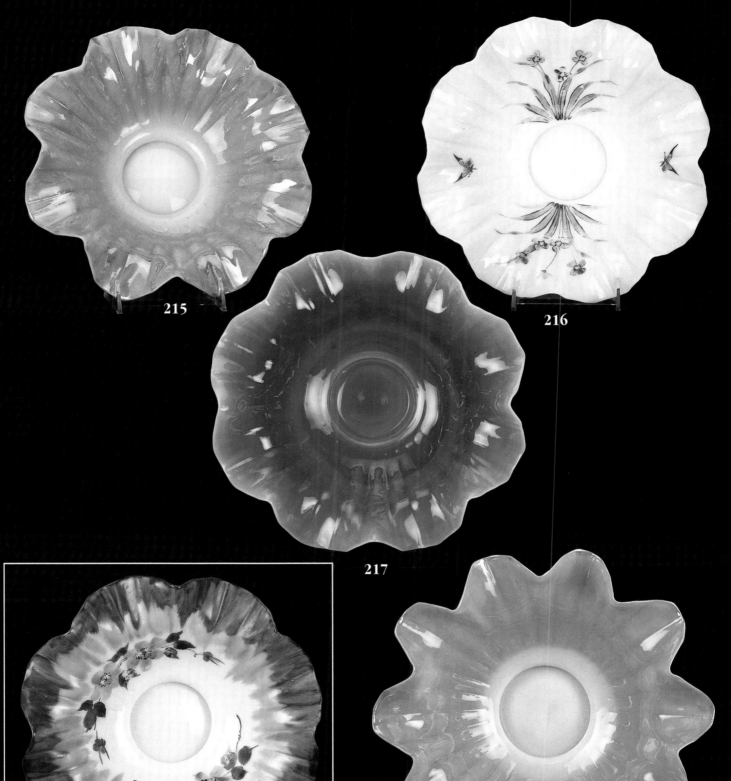

215

216

217

218

219

220

221

222

223

224   225   226

WHIMSICAL

227   228   229   230   231

232   233   234

235   236   237   238

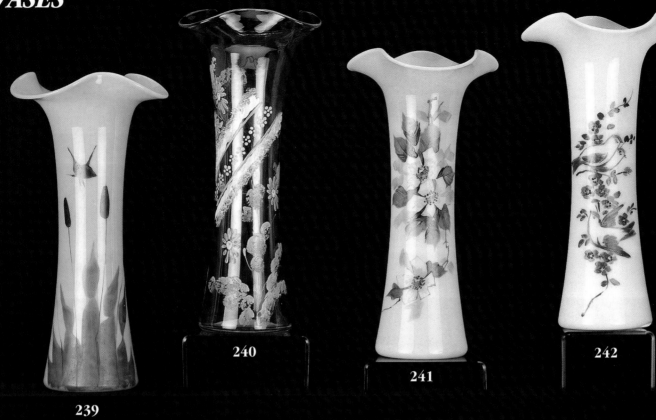

240

239

241

242

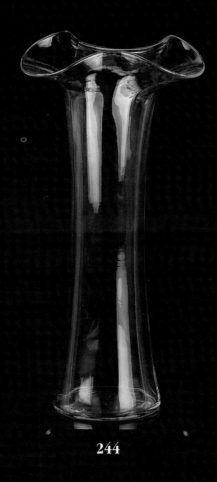

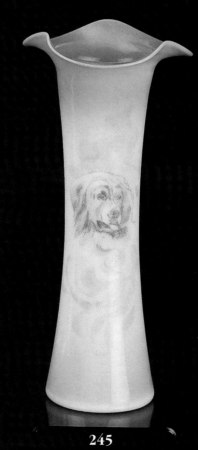

243

244

245

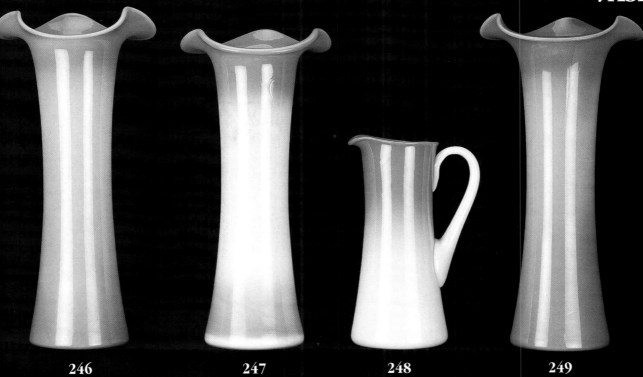

246   **247**   **248**   **249**

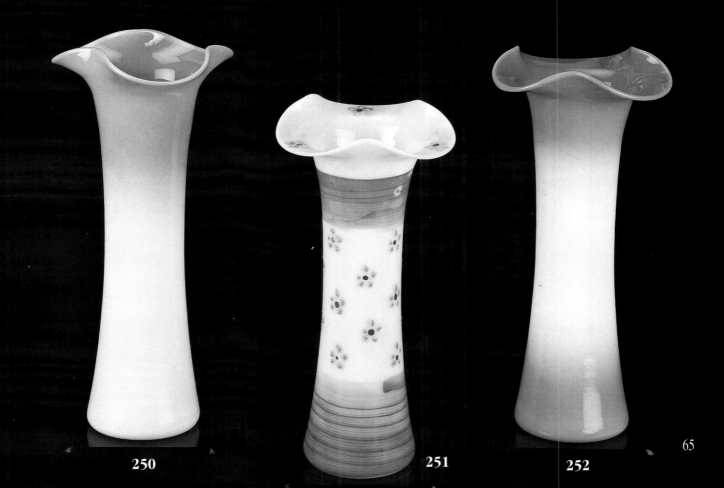

250   **251**   **252**

65

VASES

253   254   255   256

257   258   259

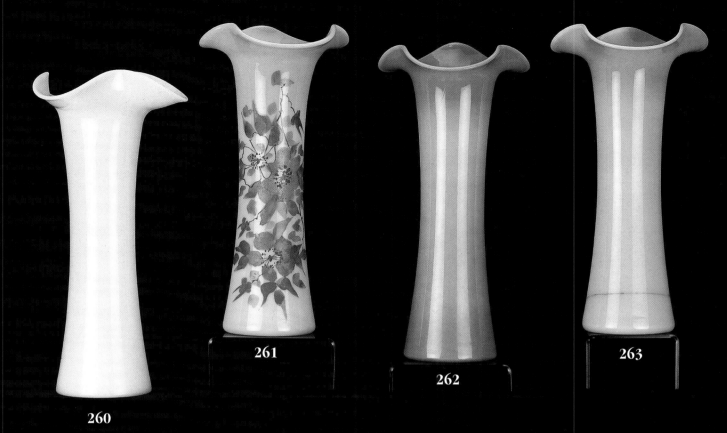

260

261

262

263

264

265

266

VASES

This painted floral motif was very popular among the decorators at Coudersport Glass. *(Bride's Basket shown courtesy of Jaybird Weimer.)*

The charming pitcher in this photograph was made from the vase mold. The pear-shaped stocking darner was a popular whimsey at many glass plants of this era. *(Pear and Vase at far right shown courtesy of Jaybird Weimer.)*

Coudersport vases were all mold-blown. The unusual vase in the center was made by enlarging the item after it was removed from the mold while still hot for reshaping. *(All vases shown courtesy of Jaybird Weimer.)*

267

268

269

270

271

WATER SETS

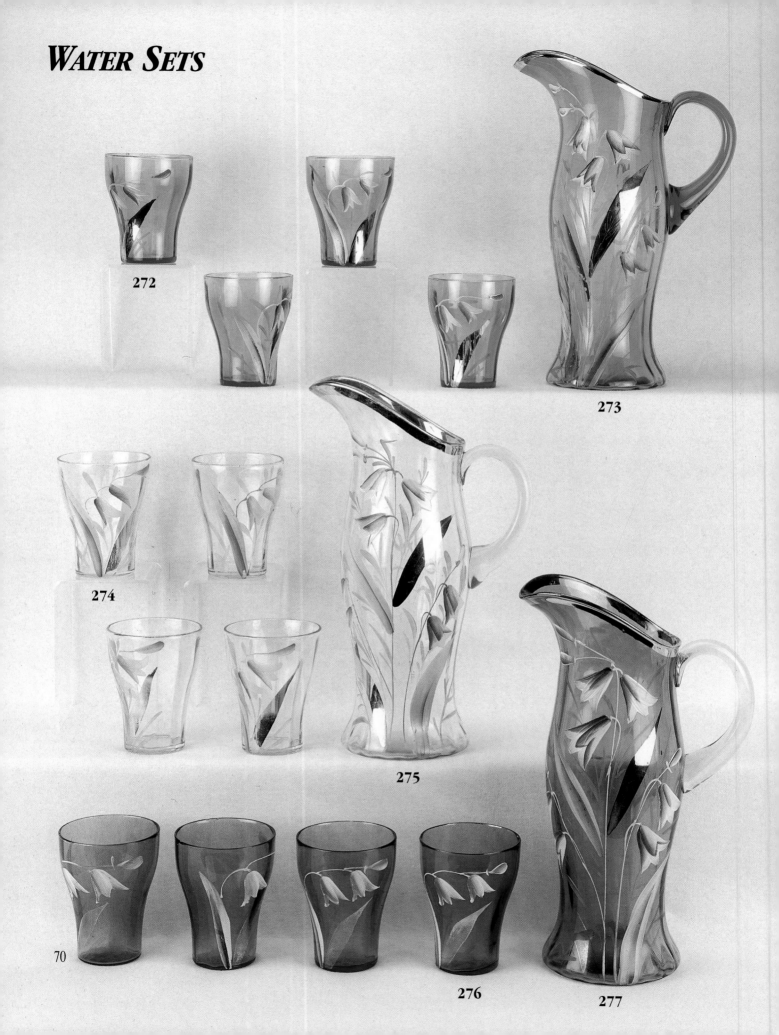

272

273

274

275

70

276

277

279

278

280

281

71

WATER SETS

(Courtesy of Scott Bruzzi)

282

283

284

285

(Courtesy of Marty Fry)

A wide variety of water sets were made at the Coudersport factory. Since most glass plants of this era also produced water sets, Coudersport pieces are very difficult to authenticate.

286

(Potter County Historical Society Museum)

287

288

289

72

(Potter County Historical Society Museum)

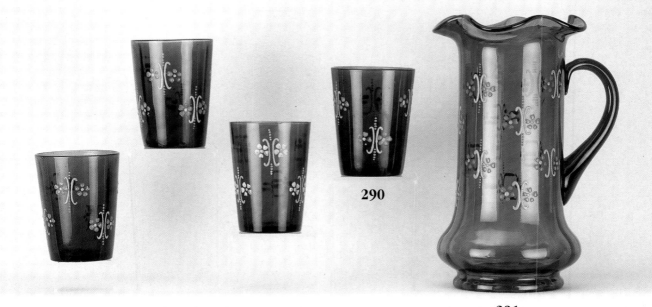

290

291

292

293

294

295

296

297

298

299

300

301

302

303

304

305

306

307

308

309

310

311

312

WINE SETS

This Communion Set was made for the Seventh Day Adventist Church in Coudersport. *(Shown courtesy of Seventh Day Adventist Church.)*

313

314

This wine set has many similarities to Coudersport Glass. Could this be one of the pressed wine sets that the Bastow Glass Company began producing in the spring of 1904, before a fire razed the factory? *(Shown courtesy of Don and Judy Young.)*

315

316

GLASS CHAIN

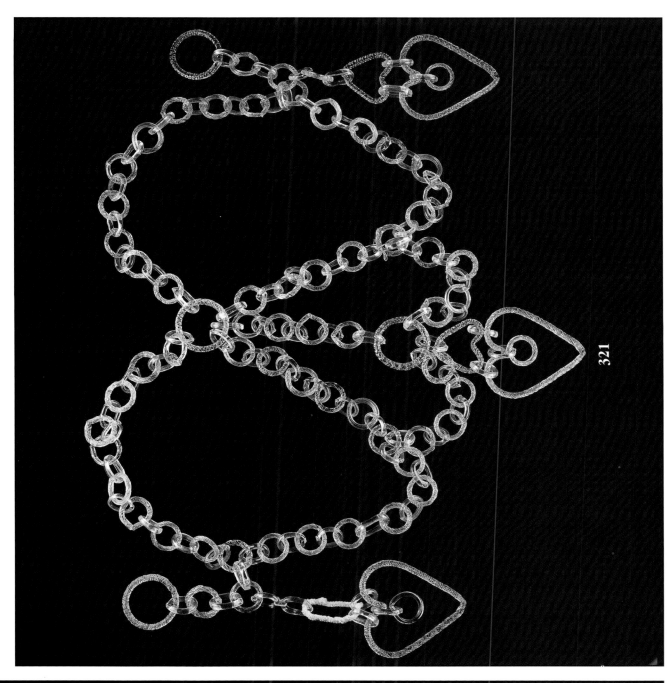

321

CANES

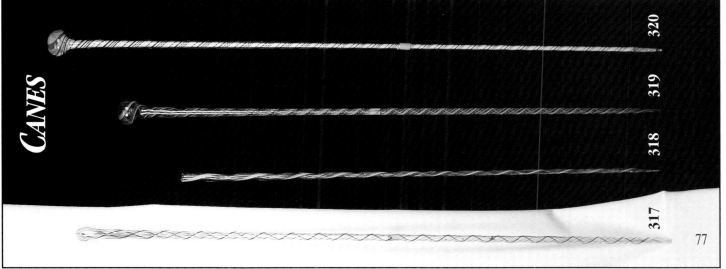

320 319 318 317

THE STAG & HOLLY DILEMMA

"Frank and I have looked at four of *Fenton's* Stag & Holly bowls. All have the Stag & Holly interior imparted by the plunger. The mould creates a three-toed bowl with 12 panels (four between each of the toes) . . . We think the amethyst opalescent is our earliest piece (1907–1908). Carnival would [come] a few years later and jade green would [date] late 1920s–early 1930s . . . Transparent pink and the light green were popular colors in the late 1920s but are virtually unknown circa 1902–1904."

--James Measell

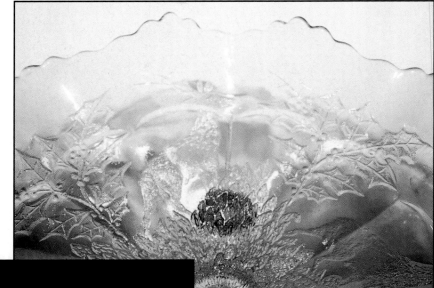

"There are four stags on the interior of each bowl. One of the stags has a pointed leaf at the ankle level of its left hind leg. This stag has four leaves (short, tall, not so tall, and tall) between its hind legs. The next stag to the right has three leaves (middle one pointed) between its hind legs. The next stag to the right has two leaves (tall and pointed) between its hind legs. The last stag has three leaves (the shortest one overlapping the leaf on the right) between its hind legs."

--James Measell

"If the pieces you find in Coudersport have maries that are just over 2" in size and the stags match those I've described, I think the pieces are far more likely to be Fenton products. As you know, when great-grandpa worked at a glass plant somewhere, folks may think every piece in the house was made there."

--James Measell

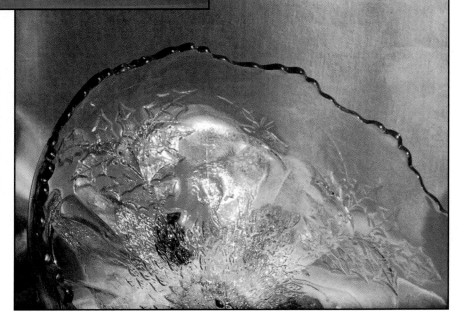

THE STAG & HOLLY DILEMMA

W as Stag & Holly made by Coudersport or Fenton? Here are the facts as I have uncovered them. In the 1970s, Floyd Bliss was a noted "authority" on Coudersport Glass by means of first finding shards at the factory site. He was also the first person to write an article on this little-known glassware. His photograph of the pink Stag & Holly bowl appeared in the November 1972 issue of *Spinning Wheel* with this caption: "Stag and Holly Pattern footed dish in transparent pale pink. Can be found in transparent green, amber and perhaps other colors as well. The mold was evidently taken from the plant when the Webbs left and later used at Fenton to produce Carnival Glass. No shards in Carnival Glass were found on the factory site."

This probably led most Coudersport collectors to include these beautiful bowls in their collections. I know that I did! While there was a measure of doubt lurking in the backs of our minds, no other company claimed to have made Stag & Holly in these transparent colors, so we continued to think that Bliss was right.

When I traveled to Fenton Art Glass several years ago, I took these bowls with me. At that time, Frank Fenton and I studied them in comparison to the carnival Stag & Holly bowls made at Fenton. We found that the maries (circular bases between the feet) on the undersides of the bowls were different. The carnival glass marie was much smaller in diameter than the transparent green and pink maries. Did this further prove Bliss's theory? It certainly did nothing to disprove it!

As this book moved closer to completion, I contacted James Measell (noted glass researcher and Associate Historian at Fenton Art Glass) and presented him with the dilemma. I decided the best thing to do was to summarize our findings for the reader.

The Stag & Holly motif on the interior of my bowls is identical to that of the Fenton bowls (indicating they were all made using the same plunger). The maries on the bowls differ slightly with the carnival measuring 1.544 inches and the jade green measuring 2.037 inches. The bottom plate in the mold could have been changed or completely new molds could have been made. My transparent pink and green bowls match the Fenton jade green bowl in the size of the marie. The maries on the bowls donated to the Potter County Historical Society by Floyd Bliss are the same two-inch size as described and, most importantly, the stags match the Fenton bowls.

Transparent pink and light green were popular colors in the late 1920s, but virtually unknown circa 1902–1904, the years that Coudersport would have produced them. Prior to 1900, Maiden's Blush decoration created a pink tint in glass, and the typical greens were emerald or olive. While the pink and green in the Stag & Holly bowls are close to Coudersport colors, various batches of glass had different shades.

Fenton made many three-toed bowls with these same feet, whereas the Coudersport factory did not make any other three-footed items. In fact, the only "footed" pieces are actually pedestal pieces.

Bob Currin, Curator of the Potter County Historical Society Museum, has repeatedly expressed his doubts about the origin of these bowls. When we sorted through the shards at the museum before writing this book, we were unable to locate any that exactly matched the Stag & Holly pattern. If Bliss did indeed have shards of these bowls, they were not given to the historical society.

These are the facts—you must draw your own conclusion. Whatever you decide, the fact remains that these bowls are very attractive and if indeed they were made by Fenton in the Twenties or Thirties, they are still very valuable items.

What do I think? Mine are moving out of my Coudersport collection!

79

REPRODUCTIONS AND OTHERS

These non-Coudersport pieces were painted by J.C. Beitler, a former decorator at the local plant.

A Japanese reproduction of the Basketweave Condiment Set (refer to the descriptions section for more information).

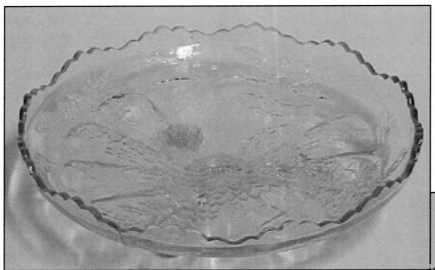

These Stag & Holly reproduction bowls are being made in transparent pink and green (refer to the descriptions section for more information).

The Coudersport Glassware Patterns

"Send for your catalogue!" (If only we could.) An advertisement for the Bastow Glass Company appeared in the April 16, 1904 edition of *China, Glass and Lamps*, inviting readers to send for a catalog of wares (see p. 27). Three weeks later, the plant was destroyed by fire.

Whether this catalog was ever printed remains to be seen. Certainly, none has been found. However, while researching the company history, I came across receipts for postcard mailings and outstanding printing charges. Did Bastow print catalogs or sales flyers, only to have them destroyed in the fire? Or, is it possible that the catalogs are stored somewhere awaiting discovery? I would like to believe the latter, but it is highly improbable (if you *do* have one stored away, please let me know!).

Coudersport glassware was not marked or identified directly on the piece. Without any catalogs or mold sketches to work from, my means of identifying patterns has been matching actual Coudersport pieces to the shards dug at the factory site. I have also talked extensively with the families of former plant workers.

Though the factory was only in operation three-and-a-half years (and only running about one-third of that time), Coudersport did produce an ample variety of patterns. The quantity of Coudersport glass that is still available is also remarkable. This chapter of the book presents an overview of patterns, and is arranged in a rough chronological fashion according to which lines were manufactured before others.

TRAILING VINE

The most familiar pattern is Trailing Vine, called "Bindweed," "Endless Vine" and even "Stinkweed" by the factory workers. Floyd Bliss called it Endless Vine in his 1972 article on Coudersport Glass which appeared in *Spinning Wheel* magazine (see page 79). Later, James H. Gaddis would name it Trailing Vine. Trailing Vine was made in covered sugar bowls, creamers, spooners, covered butter dishes and berry sets, during both the Webb and Bastow years.

SHAKERS

Salt and pepper shakers were made in three patterns to include Basketweave, Fleur de Lis and Fantasia. Basketweave was also called "Cane Woven" by Floyd Bliss (1972) and "Woven Cane" by Heacock (1976). Variations on this pattern include shakers made with a larger opening to double as mustard jars. Two shakers and a mustard fit into slots on a circular base, forming a condiment set.

Fantasia has been called "Lacy Scroll" and "Fleur de Lis with Scrolling." Fleur de Lis has been called "Fleur de Lis in Wreath" and "Fleur de Lis in Scroll." These three shaker patterns were also manufactured under both Webb and Bastow.

Collectors should not be alarmed to find that the shakers and mustards have a rough, unfinished rim. This does not detract from their value. The rims of these pieces were always covered by lids, therefore unseen, and hand-finishing work was not necessary.

POMPEII, SHADOW

Webb's own Pompeii Ware was described as "coming in a variety of shapes with a greenish-gold iridescent effect." This line was made for the "upscale" market. The Shadow Pattern was named by one of the ladies working at the Coudersport plant. She thought the cross-hatching on the top of each piece cast a shadow onto the reverse side.

Shadow is the only Coudersport pattern that was also made elsewhere. First manufactured in 1900, it is possible that the mold was removed from the factory before the fire, or that the designer was hired by another firm and reproduced the pattern.

The Northwood Glass Company advertised this pattern as their "Button Panels" in 1902 and 1903. Dugan-Diamond made it from 1907 to 1909, and possibly later.

The Coudersport factory made Shadow in four colors: white and blue opalescent are more readily available, followed by yellow opalescent and deep transparent green. I have not found any evidence that this pattern was made in green opalescent.

In his book *Opalescent Glass*, Bill Edwards states that this pattern was made only in a domed-base bowl and rose bowl. In fact, the pattern consisted of three pieces fashioned from the same mold: an open compote, a pedestal rose bowl, and a compote with straight sides. A complete set of Coudersport Shadow consists of one of each style in each of the four colors.

HEN ON NEST

The Coudersport Hen on Nest was the only item of its kind to come from this plant. The base of the piece has a very unique pattern which clearly identifies it as Coudersport. Many covered animal dishes are found with ribbed or basketweave bases, but this Hen rests on Cattails & Rushes (see page 56).

THREE FINGERS AND PANEL

Joseph Webb first produced Three Fingers and Panel during his short time at the Coudersport plant. He made creamers and sugars (both with lids) in white opaque and deep blue opaque. The pattern may have been reproduced by Westmoreland Specialty Glass Company circa 1903. It was not uncommon for Westmoreland to copy (or borrow) popular patterns of this era, and I have seen two examples of sugars with remnants of the Westmoreland company label (see page 58).

In April 1904, Harry Bastow advertised that he had "several new tradewinners" to present to the market. I believe one of these products was a line of redesigned Three Fingers and Panel items. The new pattern featured a larger creamer and covered sugar bowl, and a large covered butter dish with spooner, all pieces on a pedestal base. This pattern has been found in crystal, transparent green, custard and blue opalescent. Fewer than a dozen pieces of the new Three Fingers and Panel have ever been located, but shards found at the factory site indicate it was also made in opaque white and opaque blue.

WAFFLE & VINE

This pattern may have been the second new product that Bastow was about to release at the time of the fire, evidence by an abundance of Waffle & Vine shards found at the site of the burning. This pattern was evidently made only in an intricate pedestal dish. Among the local collectors in Coudersport, only five known examples.

VASES AND WATER SETS

In addition to the pressed glass patterns mentioned above, Coudersport also made a tall vase, a Bride's Basket, wine set, and several water sets. These were mold-blown and usually finished by hand.

The factory experimented with several one-of-a-kind pieces and a quantity of whimseys. Any whimsey item that has been authenticated is shown in the color section of this book (see pages 63 and 77).

Pressed glass items tended to have decorations that were pleasing but lacking in detail. Coudersport Glass employed local people as well as itinerant craftsman to handpaint decorations on the glassware. Collectors should be careful not to assume that an item is genuine just because its painting resembles a Coudersport decoration. While the painting *can* help to authenticate an item, many craftsmen who did the decorating often moved from factory to factory, passing along their techniques.

Descriptions for Items in Color Section

PAPERWEIGHTS (P. 34)

During a visit to the Joseph Webb Decorative Glass Co. in April 1901, a reporter from a weekly newspaper in Coudersport was told that a glassblower could mold 1,400 paperweights in a nine-hour day. (Since glassmaking is normally a team operation, it's likely that he had one or more helpers.) During this visit, it was also disclosed that shipments were made daily. The factory had an order for 1,300 gross of various products for a firm in Chicago and several large orders for items to go to the Pan-American Exposition in Buffalo, New York. We assume these shipments contained many paperweights.

The paperweights were made in a rectangular shape, measuring 2.5"–2.63" wide, 4.125"–4.375" long and between .75" and 1" high. They were clear glass with a ribbed or grooved pattern on the undersides, forming a border around the pictures that were mounted in them. After being cast, the paperweights were sold to distributors who placed scenic pictures on the backs. For this reason, the backings contain different materials.

Paperweights were also a product of the other glass houses during this period of growth in the glassmaking industry. Therefore, it is difficult to prove which ones came from the Coudersport factory. The local collectors of Coudersport Glass limit their paperweights to the style listed above. They include only those that have pictures of local interest dating from the early 1900s, and any that show the Buffalo/Niagara Falls landmarks and the Pan-American Exposition. I am sure that these paperweights were shipped to other areas of the country as well. The manner in which one limits a collection is up to each individual.

PAPERWEIGHTS (P. 35)

The paperweights in the first row show area churches and their pastors.

1. The Methodist Episcopal Church in Austin, PA (13 miles south of Coudersport). The gentleman with the nicely trimmed beard is the pastor, Rev. E. H. Whitman. This town suffered a devastating flood in 1911. *(Author's Collection)*

2. This shows the very small Union Church in Colegrove, PA which is in neighboring McKean County. The pastor is Rev. J. A. Perkins. *(Author's Collection)*

3. A View of the East River, Buffalo, New York. *(Museum Collection)*

4. The famous Kinzua Bridge is depicted on this paperweight. This railroad bridge is located about 40 miles west of Coudersport. At one time this was the highest railroad bridge in the world and considered an engineering marvel. It still stands today and is now a tourist attraction with the excursion train still taking its passengers across the bridge. *(Author's Collection)*

5. This is a view of Niagara Falls showing the original "Maid of the Mist" boat at the base of the falls. *(Author's Collection)*

6. Pan American Exposition as detailed on page 34. *(Author's Collection)*

7–8. Two views of the same section of Niagara Falls. These were apparently made from photographs taken at different angles. No. 7 has more detail than the other. *(Museum Collection)*

9. The South Side Baptist Church with the pastor Rev. Claude G. Langford in an oval in the right hand corner. *(Museum Collection)*

GLASS SHARDS (P. 36)

Without the kind of shards shown here, we may never have known what beautiful glassware had been produced during the short life of the Coudersport Glass Plant. This is a good example of the variety of shards from the factory grounds. I have tried to show the various colors and textures of glass that were found during the digging at the site.

This photograph also shows some unusual pieces. Around the Pompeii vase are shards which correspond to it. Above and to the left of the vase is a large curved piece in a cloudy

TRAILING VINE PATTERN DIMENSIONS

ITEM	HEIGHT	OUTSIDE DIAMETER	INSIDE DIAMETER
Spooner	3.875"	3.26–3.75"	2.625"
Creamer	3.875–3.91"	3.26–3.75"	2.625"
Sugar Bowl	3.84–3.875"	4.62–4.75"	3.375"
Sugar Bowl Lid	1.6" to top of knob	3.612"	3.250"
Butter Dish	1.95–1.975"	5.29–5.31"	4.375"
Butter Dish Lid	2.25" to top of knob	4.606"	4.238"
Master Berry Bowl	3.062"	3.5–3.625"	8.25"
Berry Bowl (Sauce)	1.81–1.87"	4.3–4.45"	4.125"

The inner lip on the butter and sugar is .125" wide. The inside diameter is measured below the lip on the covered items.

white color. Could this be a rim from a glass globe or lamp shade? The newspaper report printed in *The Potter County Journal* in April 1904 states that there was, among other things, a quantity of lamp shades on display. To my knowledge I do not know of a lamp shade that has been positively identified as having been made at the Coudersport factory.

Above and to the right of the vase is a clear piece of glass with a horseshoe in the center. This is the bottom of a tumbler. The search continues for an actual glass that matches this piece.

If you study these pieces closely you may be able to match one of them to an, as yet, unfound piece. We do not really know how many items were actually produced during the short life of this factory.

The publication of this book is meant to familiarize everyone with the designs from this factory in the hope that additional pieces will be found. Many of the items listed by the reporter in his trip through the plant during its operation have still not been identified.

TRAILING VINE OVERVIEW

Being the most familiar of the patterns and the most extensively produced, the Trailing Vine pattern has become synonymous with Coudersport Glass. This pattern was made in a berry set, a creamer, spooner, covered butter dish and large covered sugar bowl. From these basic pieces many novelty items and whimsies were also formed. The standard tableware pieces were made both by Webb and Bastow. The antique dealer having a piece of Coudersport Glass for sale will more than likely have a piece of the Trailing Vine pattern.

The standard dimensions of the molded pieces are listed below. Many of the top edges were hand worked after the piece was taken from the mold, therefore there will be some variation in these dimensions.

The pattern is a raised vine with leaves and blossoms running around the center of each piece. The flowers are in different stages of bloom. The larger blossom appears to be emerging from a bud and has five petals. The smaller has three petals. Located behind the larger flower there is a branch extending upward with a small two-petal bud showing. The larger diameter items show three or four flowers while the spooner or creamer will have only two with one bud.

Top and bottom edges are scalloped with five grooves in each scallop. These grooves are on the outer surface and tend to flare from the central smoother surface, which contains the vine, to the top and bottom.

The lids for the butter and sugar carry the same vine encircling a six-pointed star effect which radiates inward to the finial. This star carries the same grooved treatment as the bases. The finial appears to be a bud with the round inner section emerging from the petals in an off-centered position. The grooving treatment is evident on this knob also. Once you have seen a lid with this unusual knob you should never miss one. .

All of the Trailing Vine molds are three part. A close inspection will reveal the three mold marks. It is very evident that the opaque pieces are from the early years since the opaque components did not flow evenly to the edges. This is where the "fire" as discussed earlier is most evident.

At the time of production this was considered their cheaper line of wares. This glassware was often shipped in barrels or stacked one on top of the other for transporting. This handling, coupled with the design, has caused a lot of pieces to have chips or rough spots on the lower edges. The top edge has a much smoother, more finished feel to it, probably achieved by an extra finishing procedure.

Items listed for this pattern are measured to the largest dimension. Some variation can be expected.

TRAILING VINE SPOONERS (P. 37)

This page features a collection of Coudersport Glass Spooners in the Trailing Vine pattern. I chose this photo to start the Trailing Vine chapter because it shows the colors and types of glass produced and most of the decorating treatments which were used during the times of both Webb and Bastow.

There is no variation in the size of these spooners other than the top rim which was finished by hand. They are all 3.875" high with an inside base diameter of 2.625". The widest outside diameter at the top ranges from 3.312" to 3.75".

Coudersport Trailing Vine pattern was produced in all of the colors of glass shown plus a few others which I will cover later.

When Coudersport opaque glass is held to the light or placed under a black light, it shows an orange or yellow color resembling fire. If the glass is too thick to see through, you can tilt the item and look through the thinner glass on the edge to catch the fire effect.

10. Blue opaque with gold paint decoration. *(Leete Collection)*

11. White opaque with gold paint decoration. Coudersport collectors do not refer to this opaque white glass as milk glass, although it meets the description of old milk glass. I will refer to it only as white opaque. *(Leete Collection)*

12. Clear or crystal glass with gold paint decoration. *(Leete Collection)*

13. Transparent emerald green with gold paint decoration. *(Leete Collection)*

14. Yellow opaque with gold paint decoration. This is referred to as custard glass by most collectors and dealers. *(Leete Collection)*

15. Yellow opaque or custard, undecorated. *(Author's Collection)*

16. Transparent green, undecorated. *(Author's Collection)*

17. Clear or crystal, undecorated. *(Leete Collection)*

18. Blue opaque, undecorated. *(Leete Collection)*

19. White opaque with red decorations. This color of trim is very rare. *(Leete Collection)*

20. White opaque with blue trim. *(Leete Collection)*

21. White opaque with yellow trim. This is the hardest color of decoration to find. *(Leete Collection)*

BLUE OPAQUE AND BASKETWEAVE (P. 38)

The top photo is a portion of a Trailing Vine pattern berry set in opaque blue glass, sometimes referred to as blue milk glass. A complete berry set consists of the large 8" diameter master berry bowl and six small 4.5" diameter berry bowls. These small berry bowls are often referred to as sauce dishes. A full set is considered more valuable than the individual pieces.

On the lower left is an opaque blue condiment set in the Basketweave pattern. (See description for page 42 on Basketweave.) A set is comprised of the salt and pepper shakers with the standard small top and a mustard pot with the original hinged lid. The mustard pot is the same size as the shakers, but with a wider 1.125" diameter opening. The 6" diameter base has three 1.25" diameter indentations to hold the shakers and mustard pot.

The original handles are a simple straight rod threaded at the bottom and looped at the top to form the handle. There are two very crude leather washers located above and below the glass to form the locking devise. When in place, the handle protrudes approximately three inches above the base. These handles were sufficient but not very attractive.

Shown on the lower right is an opaque blue ladies spittoon in the Trailing Vine pattern. Yes, women of this era did chew tobacco! This unusual piece is formed from a sugar base, and is 6" high and has a 5.5" diameter at the widest point. The ridge to hold the sugar bowl lid is still visible on the top surface. Could this have been made as a gift for a new mother-in-law from one of the young glass blowers? This spittoon is probably one-of-a-kind.

TRAILING VINE, BLUE OPAQUE (P. 39)

Blue opaque is the most common color in this pattern, and I consider it one of the prettiest. All covered pieces are at a premium. The gold decoration is the only color of trim found on the standard table pieces in blue.

22. Covered sugar bowl with gold trim, including the top edges. No painting on the lid.

23. Creamer with gold trim.

24. Covered butter dish.

25. Creamer.

26. Spooner with gold trim, including top edges.

27. Small berry bowl or sauce dish.

28. Spooner.

29. Small berry bowl or sauce dish.

30. Master berry bowl.

31. Small berry bowl or sauce dish with gold trim, including top edges.

32. Pair of Fleur de Lis salt and pepper shakers.

33. Pair of Basketweave salt and pepper shakers.

34. Basketweave mustard jar with original top.

35. Basketweave condiment base.

35A. Complete Basketweave condiment set.

36. Sugar bowl lid with the burnished gold trim, rare. *(Cooney Collection)*

37. Ladies' spittoon.

38. Pair of Fantasia salt and pepper shakers.

TRAILING VINE, WHITE OPAQUE (P. 40)

White opaque is the most difficult color to find in Trailing Vine. The reason for this is not known, but as collections are built, it is the white that is the last to be completed. The difficulty in finding some of these pieces will influence their values. Here again, all covered pieces are at a premium.

39. Covered butter dish. *(Author's Collection)*

40. Covered sugar bowl. *(Museum Collection)*

41. Spooner. *(Museum Collection)*

42. Creamer. *(Museum Collection)*

43. Small berry bowl or sauce dish. *(Author's Collection)*

44. Small berry bowl or sauce dish. *(Author's Collection)*

45. Master berry bowl. *(Author's Collection)*

46. Small berry bowl or sauce dish. *(Author's Collection)*

47. Small berry bowl or sauce dish. *(Author's Collection)*

48. Pair of Fantasia salt and pepper shakers. *(Author's Collection)*

49. Basketweave mustard jar with original top. *(Museum Collection)*

50. Pair of Basketweave salt and pepper shakers. *(Museum Collection)*

51. Basketweave condiment base. *(Museum Collection)*

51A. Complete Basketweave condiment set. *(Museum Collection)*

52. Master berry bowl with drawn-in sides. *(Author's Collection)*

TRAILING VINE, BLUE DECORATED (P. 41)

Blue painting on the white Trailing Vine table pieces make a stunning display. The blue trim is among the more common of the trim colors to find, second only to gold. The white is the only color of glass that had the standard table pieces painted in anything other than gold. The covered dishes are the rarest as evidenced by the lack of a covered sugar with blue trim. The shakers at the bottom of the page have had floral decorations added wherever the pattern left enough smooth space to do this in. This is different than the standard painting of the embossed pattern.

53. Covered butter dish, no painting on the top. Painted decoration fading. *(Museum Collection)*

54. Master berry bowl, pale trim. *(Museum Collection)*

55. Creamer, fading trim colors.

56. Small berry bowl or sauce dish. *(Museum Collection)*

57. Master berry bowl, with more flare to the sides.

58. Small berry bowl or sauce dish with fading trim. *(Museum Collection)*

59. Fleur de Lis salt shaker with small flowers painted in a vertical line.

60. Fleur de Lis salt shaker, small painted flowers with the leaves on an angle.

61. Basketweave salt shaker with small flowers painted in the open space above the roping. *(Museum Collection)*

62. Fantasia salt shaker with a horizontal line of small flowers in the center. Fading paint on this shaker.

63. Fantasia salt shaker with a horizontal line of small flowers in the center. Painting is almost perfect. This shaker is one of the few that have been found with the faint markings from the Pittsburg Mold Works in reverse on the bottom. These faint marks are not indicative of the Coudersport factory, rather they are marks from the company that made the mold.

64. Covered butter dish with excellent painted trim.

BASKETWEAVE CONDIMENT SET (P. 42)

I am showing the condiment set again to give further details and to place values on the sets that may be found. Using this one set as an example, please note the different variations.

The Basketweave condiment base has two rows of caning each about .5" wide going around the sides. The roping forms the top outside edge. The top surface has four rows of caning in decreasing widths circling the handle. The handle is a threaded rod .1" thick, standing 3.125" tall. The top is formed into a loop for ease in carrying. The threaded portion goes through a small hole in the center of the glass. It is held on with a square threaded washer and a leather washer above and below the glass. This is a somewhat crude arrangement but it apparently worked.

The condiment base is very rare. It is made of very thin glass and being a relatively large item, it probably broke very easily.

The condiment set has been found in opaque white and opaque blue. I have never seen a base in the custard color but they must have been made, since the mustards are made in custard. I am not aware of any pink mustards or of a pink condiment base. If you have one please let me know, so that it can be documented. (Please be sure to see the page on reproductions for details of the Japanese version of this set.)

65. Complete condiment set as shown. All original, no trim painting.

66. Complete condiment set. Like the one pictured, but with gold-painted trim. These have been documented.

67. Complete condiment set. Like the one pictured, but with replacement tops on the shakers and a shaker top on the mustard. May be found with a replacement handle.

TRAILING VINE, GOLD DECORATED (P. 42)

Gold painting on the white Trailing Vine table pieces is the most common paint used. Note that the top edges of these pieces are trimmed in gold also. This is even more stunning.

Any shaker or mustard painted with gold trim would be rare. This Basketweave mustard jar (72.) with the gold outline on the edges of the cane is unique. This jar has a salt shaker top on it, which is a common practice. As the original tops deteriorate, they are replaced with shaker tops. The covered dishes shown here have painting on the lids. This also commands a premium price.

68. Creamer, excellent paint including top edges.

69. Spooner, excellent paint including top edges.

70. Reverse view of 69.

71. Reverse view of 68. Note the trim on the handle. This has usually worn off.

72. Basketweave mustard jar, rare gold painting (salt shaker lid).

73. Covered butter dish, painted lid. Traces of gold in the grooves of top surface of base.

74. Covered sugar bowl, excellent gold painting including lid and grooves in top surfaces of base.

TRAILING VINE, PINK DECORATED (P. 43)

Pink painting on the white Trailing Vine table pieces is difficult to find. The complete tableware set in the top row belongs to Paul Buchsen, a gift from his wife. What a treasure!

The spooner in the bottom right corner has traces of yellow paint. This is the rarest trim color. Pale rose/pink trim with gold highlights is shown on items 79, 81 and 82.

The lid for a butter dish is painted with what appears to be a deep shade of pink, giving off an almost orange cast. The green is still very good.

75. Creamer, excellent trim painting. *(Buchsen Collection)*

76. Covered sugar bowl, excellent trim painting, including lid. *(Buchsen Collection)*

77. Covered butter dish, excellent trim painting, including lid. *(Buchsen Collection)*

78. Spooner, excellent trim painting. *(Buchsen Collection)*

79. Small berry bowl or sauce dish, pale rose/pink trim with gold highlights.

80. Master berry bowl, orange cast to the trim.

81. Sugar bowl, no lid, rose/pink trim with gold highlights.

82. Spooner, pale rose/pink trim with gold highlights.

83. Fantasia salt shaker with a horizontal line of small flowers in the center. Fading paint on this shaker.

84. Fleur de Lis salt shaker with small flowers painted in a vertical lines. *(Museum Collection)*

85. Butter dish lid, orange cast to the trim, fading. *(Museum Collection)*

86. Spooner, yellow trim, fading, very rare. *(Museum Collection)*

TRAILING VINE, CUSTARD (P. 44)

Custard Trailing Vine is very collectible both by custard glass collectors and Coudersport collectors. Gold is the only painted trim on the basic tableware pieces.

Shown on this page is a Trailing Vine novelty dish with the signature of Gomer Hughes. Hughes was a decorator at the Coudersport plant. The reverse of this piece is shown on page 50 with the novelties. This piece is in the Potter County Historical Society Museum and is the only item with a signature documented to date. (The number is a museum code.)

87. Covered butter dish, excellent trim painting, on top edges also, including lid.

88. Creamer, good trim painting, on top edges also.

89. Spooner, excellent trim painting, on top edges also.

90. Master berry bowl, good trim painting, on top edges also, though starting to wear off.

TRAILING VINE, CUSTARD (P. 45)

Custard Glass Trailing Vine tableware pieces were some of the first items from this plant to be pictured in a reference book. William Heacock shows six pieces in his book, *Encyclopedia of Victorian Colored Pattern Glass, Book 4: Custard Glass, From A to Z*, which was published in 1976. The custard glass Trailing Vine is one of the more readily available colors to collect. Anyone starting a new collection will do well in choosing this color.

91. Small berry bowl or sauce dish.

92. Master berry bowl.

93. Spooner, hanging by chains. (Author's note: This is the way that I purchased this item. Someone had been very creative in the use of this spooner.)

94. Covered sugar bowl.

95. Creamer.

96. Covered butter dish.

97. Single Fleur de Lis salt shaker.

98. Pair of Fleur de Lis salt and pepper shakers.

99. Single Fantasia salt shaker.

100. Pair of Fantasia salt and pepper shakers.

101. Single Basketweave salt shaker.

102. Basketweave mustard jar, with a shaker top.

103. Pair of Basketweave salt and pepper shakers.

TRAILING VINE, TRANSPARENT GREEN (PP. 46-47)

Trailing Vine tableware pieces in any of the transparent colors are rare. Of the transparent colors the green is the most readily available. Much of this was painted in gold. All painted items on this page have the top edges painted.

A characteristic of the transparent glass is the different shades or tints as evidenced in this color photograph. There does not seem to be any preference of tints among collectors, though the deep shades are more scarce.

104. Sugar bowl, unpainted, no lid, true green tint. *(Museum Collection)*

105. Covered butter dish, good gold trim on dish and lid, deep tint.

106. Covered sugar bowl, green trim, true green tint.

107. Creamer, unpainted, lighter green tint.*(Museum Collection)*

108. Spooner, unpainted, lighter green tint.*(Museum Collection)*

109. Spooner, good gold trim, lighter green tint.

110. Small berry bowl or sauce dish, good gold trim, true green tint.

111. Spooner, unpainted, deep green tint.

112. Creamer, good gold trim, deep green tint.

113. Small berry bowl or sauce dish, unpainted, true green tint. *(Museum Collection)*

114. Master berry bowl, deep green tint, turned-in sides.

115. Small berry bowl or sauce dish, good gold trim, true green tint.

RARE TRAILING VINE (P. 48)

This color photograph shows some of the choicest glassware in the Trailing Vine pattern. The pink glass items pictured in the top photo are by far the hardest to find.

The small amber vase is the only Trailing Vine item I am aware of that was made in this color. This particular one has a trace of opalescence at the top rim. There have been others without this opalescence. By grouping together the crystal berry dishes in the lower photo, the difference in tints is plain to see.

116. Small berry bowl or sauce dish, transparent pink, unpainted. *(Cooney Collection)*

117. Master berry bowl, transparent pink, unpainted. *(Museum Collection)*

118. Small berry bowl or sauce dish, opaque pink, good gold trim. *(Museum Collection)*

119. Amber vase, traces of opalescence. *(Museum Collection)*

TRAILING VINE, CRYSTAL (P. 49)

The different tints in the glass are not as evident here but they are included in the descriptions. Due to the difficulty in finding transparent pieces you will notice some of these are a little rough on the bottom. Most collectors retain a chipped item in the transparent pieces until it can be replaced with a better one.

120. Small berry bowl or sauce dish, unpainted, clear crystal.

121. Master berry bowl, unpainted, deep cast to glass. *(Cooney Collection)*

122. Small berry bowl or sauce dish, unpainted, clear crystal.

123. Sugar bowl, gold trim, some missing. *(Cooney Collection)*

124. Sugar bowl, unpainted. *(Museum Collection)*

125. Sugar bowl, good gold trim. *(Museum Collection)*

126. Spooner, unpainted, pale cast to glass. *(Museum Collection)*

127. Covered butter dish, good gold trim on dish and lid. *(Museum Collection)*

128. Spooner, unpainted.

TRAILING VINE NOVELTIES (P. 50)

Many novelty items were made using the Trailing Vine molds. While the piece was still hot, it could be bent, stretched, fluted, crimped or flattened according to the whim of the glass blower. A popular shape in the Coudersport plant was the tri-cornered petal design. This was among the easiest to form and also one of the most graceful.

Opaque novelty pieces usually had flowers painted on the top surfaces. The transparent ones were sometimes refired to bring out an opalescent effect.

These methods of production made each item at least a little different. It may only be in the amount of opalescence, the degree to which a section is flared or crimped, or the style of decoration used. The individuality of these novelties make them a joy to collect.

In the listings that follow, the mold used to form the original piece is identified. This allows the reader to use the basic Trailing Vine dimensions on page 84 to identify the base of each piece.

129. Crystal opalescent, six scallops on the top edge. Opalescence makes glass look cloudy. Spooner mold.

130. Crystal opalescent, six scallops on the top edge. A "pleating" effect on the inside surface. Sugar mold. *(Museum Collection)*

131. Crystal opalescent. Top has been flattened and then two sides pulled back in. Spooner mold.

132. Custard glass formed into the popular tri-cornered petal style. Top surface painted with blue and rust flowers, good detail. Spooner mold. (Note: This is the novelty shown on page 44 with the Gomer Hughes signature. *(Museum Collection)*

133. Blue opaque glass formed into the tri-cornered style, red flowers painted on top. Spooner mold.

134. White opaque glass formed into the tri-cornered style, rust-colored flower painted on the top, some fading. Spooner mold. *(Cooney Collection)*

135. Custard glass formed into the tri-cornered style, rust-colored flower painted on the top. Spooner mold.

136. Custard glass, sides drawn in at three places. Master berry mold. *(Cooney Collection)*

137. Transparent blue opalescent glass, formed into the tri-cornered style. The thickness of the outer rim is evident in this view. Spooner mold.

TRAILING VINE, OPALESCENT (P. 51)

The only opalescent pieces made in the Trailing Vine pattern are the novelties. A wide variety of shapes and sizes were made and they are relatively plentiful. Most collectors are thrilled to find one of these adorable dishes in a style that they are missing.

Here is a curious finding: The beautiful blue transparent and vaseline glass used in these novelties are not found in the standard tableware items. Was there some reason that these colors was not used for the standard tableware?

The transparent blue is used in the vases and brides baskets, but the yellow shows up only in opalescent. In these listings also the mold used to form the original piece is identified. The basic Trailing Vine dimensions on page 86 can be used to identify the base of each piece. Heights and diameters of the hand-worked areas are omitted due to the extreme variances.

138. Vaseline opalescent, six scallops on the top edge. A dark line of glass is found in the opalescent area. Sugar mold. *(Museum Collection)*

139. Vaseline opalescent, shortened piece with a "pleating" effect on the inside surface. Sugar mold. Very rare. *(Museum Collection)*

140. Vaseline opalescent, eight deep scallops on top edge. Sugar mold. *(Cooney Collection)*

141. Vaseline opalescent, six scallops on top edge, pleating on the inside. Sugar mold.

142. Vaseline opalescent, three extra deep scallops on top edge, pleating extending half-way down the bowl. Sugar mold. Unusual. *(Museum Collection)*

143. Vaseline opalescent, drawn in tightly to form a small neck, then flared out in the tri-cornered design. Resembles a small vase. Spooner mold. Scarce. *(Cooney Collection)*

144. Vaseline opalescent, formed into the tri-cornered design. Each petal is turned back in at the very edge. Spooner mold.

145. Blue opalescent glass, deep blue tint, pleated top, flattened, two sides lifted up and pinched inward. Spooner mold.

146. Blue opalescent glass, deep blue tint, spread out with two sides slightly raised and pinched inward. Spooner mold. *(Museum Collection)*

147. Blue opalescent glass, deep blue tint, three scallops on top edge, faint pleating. Spooner mold. *(Museum Collection)*

148. Blue opalescent glass, formed into the tri-cornered style. Each petal is slightly pinched inward. Spooner mold.

149. Blue opalescent glass, top flattened and raised into six low scallops, heavy opalescence on outer edge. Spooner mold. Scarce. *(Cooney Collection)*

150. Blue opalescent glass, drawn in tightly to form a small neck, then flared out forming six small scallops. Resembles a small vase. Spooner mold. Scarce. *(Thomas Collection)*

151. Blue opalescent glass, six scallops on the top edge, a dark line of glass around the outer edge of the opalescent area. Sugar mold.

152. Blue opalescent glass, deep blue tint, three scallops on the top edge, minimal opalescence. Spooner mold. *(Cooney Collection)*

153. Blue opalescent glass, eight scallops on the top edge, heavy outer rim of opalescence. Sugar mold. Unusual.

SHADOW (P. 52)

Local tradition has it that the Shadow pattern was named by one of the ladies working at the plant. She felt that the cross hatching or quilting on the inside gave a shadow effect on the reverse side.

Like its name, this pattern has a shadowy past. Coudersport collectors have believed that Shadow was first made in Coudersport in 1900, and that it was later produced by the Northwood and Dugan/Diamond glass companies. This pattern was named Button Panels by glass researcher Marion T. Hartung.

In *Dugan/Diamond: The Story of Indiana, Pennsylvania Glass* by Heacock, Measell, and Wiggins (1993), an ad is reprinted from the Spring 1899 Butler Brothers catalog that shows a

Button Panels piece among a group of items. This evidence indicates that the Shadow/Button Panel pattern predates the Coudersport factory.

Since this pattern is strongly associated with Coudersport by shard evidence and local history, we can only speculate how other plants produced this pattern. Harry Bastow's close association with Northwood might explain why both companies made essentially the same pattern.

Due to the fact that production of this pattern has continued, a collector should check the pieces carefully. Look for the usual details of old glass: imperfections, foreign matter in the glass, wear on the bottoms or traces of water stains. I have found no definite way to attribute these older examples to either Coudersport or Northwood.

The Coudersport factory made this pattern in four colors. The white and blue opalescent colors are the more readily available, followed by the vaseline opalescent and the deep transparent green. I have not found any evidence that this pattern was made in green opalescent in the Coudersport plant.

Coudersport Glass collectors search for three styles of this pedestal dish. It was made in an open compote style, a pedestal rose bowl and the same style with straight sides. (Author's note: In Bill Edwards' book on opalescent glass, he states that it was made only in the domed base bowls and the rose bowls.) A complete set for the Coudersport collector would consist of one each of these three styles in each of the four Coudersport colors.

The pattern consists of a pedestal base with small horizontal rings covering the outside of the dish approximately two thirds of the way up. At this point the glass is smooth and flows into either the pleated tops of the rose bowl types or the flared scallops of the open compotes. There are four ribs evenly spaced and overlaying the horizontal rings. These ribs have a raised treatment on them. The inside has a quilted pattern. This is what that women long ago thought caused a shadow effect.

154. Crystal opalescent, rose bowl shape.

155-156. Crystal opalescent, open compote style, two views.

157. Crystal opalescent, straight-sided compote.

SHADOW (P. 53)

158. Blue opalescent, straight-sided compote.

159. Blue opalescent, open compote.

160. Blue opalescent, rose bowl shape.

161. Blue opalescent, deep blue tint, rose bowl shape.

162. Transparent green, open compote.

163. Transparent green, rose bowl shape.

164. Transparent green, straight-sided compote.

165. Opalescent green, open compote. Not believed to be Coudersport, included only for comparison. Note the pale green color, not consistent with any shards at the site. No value will be given.

166. Green transparent glass, rose bowl style, teal shade, very questionable. No value will be given.

167. Vaseline opalescent, rose bowl shape.

168. Vaseline opalescent, open compote.

169. Vaseline opalescent, straight-sided compote.

SALT & PEPPER SHAKERS (P. 54)

The three salt and pepper shaker designs produced at the Coudersport plant are shown on this page.

The Fantasia pattern was blown into a three-part mold. One Fleur de Lis is located in the downward position and one is extending up in the center of each section. These are joined together with a lacy pattern of scrolling. The shaker is in an almost triangular shape.

The Fleur de Lis pattern has three larger Fleur de Lis in the upright position, each surrounded by delicate scrolling. The shape of this shaker is reminiscent of a small bell. These were also blown into a three-part mold.

The Basketweave pattern has five rows of caning in a woven pattern going horizontally around the shakers and mustards. Each row is approximately 1/4" wide. Above the top row is a rope pattern about 1/8" thick. These are shaped like a small barrel. The chart below lists measurements taken to the largest dimension. Some variation can be expected.

Coudersport made shakers in opaque glass only. The colors produced were white, custard (yellow), blue and pink. The other companies of this era made shakers in colors that closely resemble these. Color alone cannot identify shakers as having been made in Coudersport.

It is apparent here and throughout this book that there was a great variation in the shades of color of these shakers. The Fantasia shakers in the top photo are a good example of this.

The photo of the pink Fleur de Lis shakers also shows the variation in shades as well as the marbling that is found on many of the rare pink shakers. There does not appear to be any value differences in the shades of shakers except the marbled ones which are much more valuable.

The Basketweave condiment set has been found in white and blue. Although I have not seen a custard set, I believe they must have been made. A pink set would be extremely rare.

There was a substantial number of these shakers made. As the bottle digging era was taking place in the late sixties and early seventies, many of these shakers began to turn up. Finding a shaker from the local plant has started many collectors on their quest for more Coudersport Glass.

It hasn't been too many years ago since work was being done under one of the Main Street buildings in Coudersport when a large number of these shakers were found. Could this have been where Allen's Department Store was located? Were these the shakers that they were unable to sell after the demise of the Bastow plant?

Note: See page 78 for a photo of the reproduction condiment set.

170. Fantasia shaker in a deep blue tint.

171. Fantasia shaker in a light blue tint.

172. Fantasia shaker in a medium shade of blue.

SHAKER PATTERN DIMENSIONS

ITEM	HEIGHT	OUTSIDE DIAMETER	INSIDE DIAMETER
Fantasia Shaker	2.4–2.612"	2.25"	3.26–3.75"
Fleur de Lis Shaker	2.4–2.612"	3.26–3.75"	2.625"
Basketweave Shaker	2.4–2.612"	2.1"	.725"
Basketweave Mustard	2.4–2.612"	2.1"	1.04–1.07"
Basketweave Condiment Base	1.375"	6.125"	5.79"

173. Fantasia shaker in a deep blue tint.

174. Fantasia shaker in white opaque.

175. Fleur de Lis shaker in white opaque.

176. Fleur de Lis shaker in white opaque.

177. Fantasia shaker in white opaque.

RARE SHAKERS (P. 55)

This grouping of pink shakers shows the various shadings that were produced. Pink is one of the hardest colors to find, so they are considered very rare. Some of these shakers show a mixture of white and pink. It is believed that this was really due to poor mixing of the glass or else the adding of pink color components at the end of a run to make these special shakers as workers' whimsies or "take home" items. Whatever the reason, these multicolored shakers are highly sought after.

No. 195 is a pink satin glass shaker in the Fleur de Lis pattern. This is the only piece of satin glass that has been found in a Coudersport pattern. Since Webb was known for his work in satin glass, I believe this was probably made by him as an experimental piece.

The shaker lids shown here are a mixture of original and replacement items. Collectors prefer the old lids if possible, but since so many have deteriorated, any lids that appear old are used when needed. All of these shakers have a rough unfinished rim as shown in item No. 196. As explained earlier, this is the way they were made and it does not detract from their value.

178. Basketweave shaker in shades of white.

179-180. Fleur-de-Lis shakers in pink opaque.

181. Basketweave shaker with purple cast.

182. Basketweave shaker in purple cast with shades of white.

183. Fantasia shaker with large mixture of white.

184. Fantasia shaker in true pink.

185. Fleur-de-Lis shaker in pink opaque with white painting.

186-187. Fantasia shakers in true pink opaque.

188-189. Basketweave shakers with purple cast.

190. Basketweave shaker in pink opaque.

191-192. Basketweave shakers with some white.

193. Fleur-de-Lis shaker in true pink opaque.

194. Fleur-de-Lis shaker in white marbled glass.

195. Fleur-de-Lis shaker in satin glass.

196. Fleur-de-Lis shaker in white marbled glass.

197. Fleur-de-Lis shaker in pink opaque.

198. Fleur-de-Lis shaker in pink opaque.

HEN ON NEST, CATTAIL & RUSHES (P. 56)

This charming hen on the nest is the only figural item produced at the Coudersport factory. Identification of these is quite easy. The hen has her head turned to the side and the tail is split. There are two eggs visible in the front, one small one in the back, and a larger egg at either side of her tail feathers.

The base or nest is a design of cattails and rushes reaching up towards the rope trim that encircles the top edge. The cattail is repeated four times around the base, two in front and two in back. The rushes cross over themselves at four places.

These hens are a good example of the opaque or milk glass that was being made in the early 1900's. The large view clearly shows the lack of color in the edges of the item. This is characteristic of the old opaque glass. Holding a Coudersport hen to the light will show a great deal of fire which gives an opalescent effect. On the ones that I have had, the top is almost transparent and on the base the fire always shows through the roping.

The hen in No. 200 shows traces of paint on the comb. Many of these covered hen dishes had the combs painted.

The base is an oval approximately 3.75" X 5.75" at the roping. It is roughly 1.75" high. The top is an oval 3.25" X 4.75" and is 2.875" tall at the tail. With the two pieces together, the overall height is roughly 4.5". Be sure that the top and bottom fit together well. It is almost impossible to use a different hen on a Coudersport base. They will not fit.

199. Hen on Nest in white opaque.

200. Hen on Nest, with traces of paint on the tail. *(Museum Collection)*

GLASS SHARDS (P. 57)

This page shows another grouping of shards from the factory. The actual items matched to the various shards is the main means of identification that Coudersport Glass researchers have used.

The Basketweave pattern shards in the upper left hand corner match the blue condiment set base and the opaque pink shaker. Below the white Trailing Vine spooner are shards of this pattern. The top right corner shows a Waffle & Vine compote among some of the largest shards from the site.

In the middle row are two pieces of glass from the bottom of tumblers. Beside these we have placed a tumbler showing the formation of a star or pinwheel which is found on the base of many of the Coudersport Glass tumblers. The next grouping shows three Fantasia pattern salt shakers with the corresponding shards.

In the lower left corner is the white opaline water jug which fades from white to pink. The pieces around it match the jug and also the vases that were made in this same glass. In the right bottom corner is another grouping of larger shards. In the center of these is a Three Fingers and Panel spooner which coincides with these pieces. Below the spooner are three finials matching the Three Fingers and Panels lids.

THREE FINGERS AND PANEL CREAM & SUGAR SETS (P. 58)

These sets of creamers and sugar bowls were the original Three Fingers and Panel pieces. Made in white and blue opaque glass, most of these were trimmed in gold. The gold used on these items has the burnished appearance. Some had flowers painted in various colors in the panels.

The creamer and sugar both had lids. It is believed that these were sold to condiment companies to be filled with their mustard, peanut butter and similar food items. A cardboard cover was placed on the inner lip to seal in the contents.

The embossed pattern has two sets of three fingers on each side surrounding a panel which is edged with scrolling. These fingers are separated by two small rows of beading. Above the fingers at each end is an area of scrolling. The top edges are scalloped.

The lids have fourteen tapered bulges divided by beading. The handle is comprised of two ridged sections that are arched and joined together with a single ball in the center. The beading is repeated on the outer edge of the ridged arches. The total effect is similar to a crown.

This pattern is oval shaped and has a small oval pedestal base. The pedestal is 3.12" by 2.19". The body is an oval 3" x 4.25". They are 3.5" high excluding the creamer lip. With the tops in place the total height is 4.75".

Since these were later made by Westmoreland Glass, it is hard to differentiate between theirs and the originals from the Coudersport plant. Remember that the glass used in Coudersport shows a lot of the 'fire' in it, especially where the colors have not flowed to the edges. The later ones are more dense in these areas.

201. Creamer with lid in white opaque.

202. Sugar bowl with lid in white opaque.

203. Sugar bowl with lid in blue opaque.

204. Creamer with lid in blue opaque.

THREE FINGERS AND PANEL PATTERN, RARE (P. 59)

The large quantity of shards of this pattern lead me to believe that this was one of the new selections that Bastow was about to release to the public. Or was he already producing this attractive line? As more pieces of this are located, maybe these mysteries will be solved.

Harry Bastow and his designers appear to have taken the original Three Fingers and Panel design and enlarged upon it. By also adding some smaller more intricate detailing they have made these pieces quite elegant.

Apparently this pattern was made in a tableware set consisting of a large covered butter, covered sugar, spooner and creamer—all with low pedestals. The sugar bowl has no handle but it can be differentiated from the spooner by way of the lip to hold the lid and the larger diameter pedestal. The creamer is the same size as the spooner. (I hope that there is a berry set somewhere waiting to be found.)

The pedestal diameters are 3" on the creamer and spooner, 3.61" on the sugar bowl and 3.812" on the butter dish. The spooner is 4.75" tall, and the sugar bowl is the same. Adding the lid to the sugar bowl makes it 7.61" tall overall. The creamer is 5" high to the top of the spout and the butter dish is 2.75" tall without the lid. The diameter of the butter dish is 8" and the stately lid brings the overall height to 7".

The embossed pattern formed by the mold has three fingers flaring out slightly as they run from the pedestal up the sides of the piece. The pedestal and the top rim have six scallops, three with the finger design alternating with three which are plain. These fingers are divided by two rows of beading. On either side of the fingers is a feather styled outline also reaching to the same height as the fingers. Attached to the side of this is a small line of scallops encircling the panel. Above each of the three sets of fingers is a dainty leaf and scroll design. This leaf and scroll design is repeated three times on the top edge of the butter dish.

The lids are easy to identify by the finial. There are three rows of vertical beading joined together at the top. This gives it a crown effect. The ribbed handle on the creamer is almost identical to the handle used on the Trailing Vine pattern.

There have been items or shards located to show that Three Fingers and Panel was made in crystal, transparent green, transparent blue, custard and white opaque. A crystal creamer painted with colored flowers belongs to one of the local collectors. This wide assortment of colors and trim shown in the few pieces that have been found so far leads me to believe this pattern is another example of "what might have been."

The three crystal items in the top row were found in a local shop almost thirty years ago. The antique dealer assured Mina Cooney that these were from the local plant . Not entirely sure that they were, she took a chance and bought them all for thirty dollars. What a find!

This pattern is still very scarce, and I hope by documenting this design it will enable more pieces to be located. See page 75 for more information on this pattern.

205. Covered sugar bowl in crystal. *(Cooney Collection)*

206. Creamer in crystal. *(Cooney Collection)*

207. Covered butter dish in crystal. *(Cooney Collection)*

208. Base of a butter dish in custard glass.

209. Sugar bowl base in transparent blue with added opalescence. Reworked to form an open compote.

210. Transparent green spooner. *(Museum Collection)*

WAFFLE & VINE, RARE (P. 60)

This beautiful pattern is one of my favorites. Due to the fact that there has never been any documentation, it was never named. I named it Waffle & Vine after the patterns depicted in the alternating panels in the top of the dish.

This has only been found in the pedestal dish or compote shown here. It is 4.195" tall at its highest point. The base is 3.25" in diameter and the top extends to almost 6.5" at its widest point. Three ribbed risers which support the bowl are turned outward in the scroll fashion. The embossed pattern is on the underside of the dish with a smooth top surface.

Looking down on the top, you see twelve triangular shaped panels with the narrow points in the center and flaring out to an opalescent tipped edge. Six of these panels have a waffle style pattern surrounded by scrolling. The other six panels show a vine twisting gracefully upward. The two styles alternate and each comes to a point at the outer edge. The forming of the bowl results in three lower sections and three upward sections.

The many shards at the site show that these were made in a wide variety of colors. To date, there have been compotes found of this pattern in transparent green, crystal and a beautiful transparent aqua, all with opalescent edges.

This pattern incorporates many of the details used in the other products from this factory. Could it be that this pattern was made into other pieces that we have not yet found? If the theory is correct that this was one of the new patterns due to be released at the time of the fire, just think "what might have been."

Since there have been so few of these pedestal dishes found, they are at a premium. There have only been two recorded sales of these in the last few years—one at auction for $750.00 followed by a private purchase at $500.00. Since these were both purchased by avid collectors, these values may be somewhat inflated.

Note: Both of my examples of this dish have four faint circles in a line between two of the risers. This looks as if it is an imperfection in the mold, but these circles would stand to clearly identify a piece as being authentic.

211. Open compote in light transparent blue opalescent. *(Author's Collection)*

212. Open compote in light transparent green opalescent. *(Author's Collection)*

213. Open compote in light transparent green opalescent. *(Museum Collection)*

214. Open compote in crystal opalescent. *(Darrin Collection)*

BRIDE'S BASKETS (P. 61)

The Brides Baskets that have been authenticated as Coudersport Glass are very similar in shape. The base diameter is 3.6" and the overall diameter varies from 10.5" to 11". Since these pieces were hand finished, there are no two exactly alike.

The baskets, or bowls as they are sometimes called, have either eight or ten scallops. There is a pleating design that runs from the outer rim to about three quarters of an inch from the base. There are no mold lines that circle the bowl. These bowls are some of the thinnest pieces of glass that came from the Coudersport plant.

The inside surfaces of items 215 and 219 have a gold luminescent finish that closely resembles the Muranese line which Joseph Webb perfected at New Martinsville. A portion of the description of Muranese contains the wording, "The inside is burnished gold of brilliant luster, with iridescent effects." This describes the inside of these bowls exactly! However, the shape of the Muranese line of wares is different, having a crimped or 'pie crust' edge on their Bride's Baskets. Since Webb started at New Martinsville in December of 1901, just one year after leaving the Coudersport plant, it appears that he had the ability to make this type of glass during his short stay at Coudersport.

These Bride's Baskets are very scarce and their values reflect this fact. The examples shown on this page have different characteristics.

215. White opaline glass that shades to a very deep pink.

216. White opaline glass painted with delicate flowers and two small birds. *(Cooney Collection)*

217. Transparent blue as found in the Trailing Vine opalescent novelty dishes. This piece is very thin and has a trace of opalescence at the outer edges.

218. White opaline bowl painted with shades of green around the edges. The five petaled flower decor, which was used on many Coudersport items, has been painted in the central area. *(Weimer Collection)*

219. White opaline glass that shades to a very deep pink, as in item 215. *(Museum Collection)*

PUNCHED AND DRAPED JUGS (P. 62)

These charming water jugs have been donated to the Potter County Historical Society. They are 4.5" to 4.75" high and 4" in diameter at the widest point.

The fact that there have not been any recorded sales makes it difficult to place a value on these items. Should any more of these jugs turn up, they would be extremely valuable to serious Coudersport glass collectors.

220. Opaline glass that fades from a deep pink to a true white. Bernard Hauber, a well- known Coudersport resident, left this beautiful pink and white jug to the museum after his death. This piece closely resembles the Peachblow glass that Joseph Webb was noted for.

221 & 222. Two crystal jugs in the draped pattern. These examples were left to the museum by Floyd Bliss. Note that item 222 has a much more pronounced drape in the glass than item 221.

223. Decorated amber jug with an applied handle and spout. This was donated by Marcia B. Newitt. The painting on this jug was done by her father, Mr. J. C. Beitler. Beitler was a noted decorator who worked for Webb during 1900. The transparent amber glass is one of the colors that Webb was working with at the time of his departure from Coudersport. This hand-painted floral design is one of the better examples of the work of the decorating department. The painting is of blue Forget Me Nots and green leaves with gold outlining on the top and bottom edges. Perhaps Beitler made this for someone special since the painting is so well done.

POMPEII WARE AND WHIMSIES (P. 63)

The three vases in the top row are what is believed to be the "Pompeii Ware" that Joseph and Fitzroy Webb were marketing in mid-1900. This line was described as being made in a variety of shapes with a greenish gold iridescent effect.

These vases are composed of transparent green glass with a heavy gold outer finish which has a slightly rough texture. They are 10" to 11" high and are 6" to 6.5" in diameter.

224. Pompeii ware with gold running in vertical lines which join together at the base.

225. Pompeii ware with a speckled effect all over the gold finish.

226. Pompeii ware with a gold line pattern like item 224.

The whimsies on this page are almost all one-of-a-kind items or had very limited production. Some of these were probably experimental pieces that never made it to the production stage for one reason or another. Obviously, it is particularly difficult to assign values to these items.

227. Fantasia salt shaker in custard glass which decorator J.C. Beitler had taken home. It has a covering of various colors of glass, including the gold which is evident on the Pompeii ware. (Note, this is definitely a new top.)

228. Basketweave shaker in custard glass which has been covered with chips of glass and refired.

229. Trailing Vine vase in amber which is also shown and described as item 119 on page 48.

230. Amber bud vase that was another of the items given to the historical society by Mr. Beitler's daughter. The neck of this piece has a purple shading with golden highlights. This was probably an experimental item.

231. Amber bowl with a gold crackled overlay. This was also given by the Beitler family. It is very different from any other Coudersport glassware. There have not been any other examples found to match this one.

232. Sock darner in end-of-day glass. These are wonderful keepsakes but keep in mind that all of the glassworkers in the factories of this time made this type of whimsy. Unless a person can be completely sure of the origin of these articles, there is no way to accurately match a whimsy with a specific manufacturer.

233. Sock darner in the shape of a pear. This particular one was found just below the surface at a dump in Coudersport. The glass is very fragile and it is amazing that it was found intact. The white opaline glass with the pink shadings similar to Peachblow make it a stunning whimsy (Note: These can occasionally be found in antique shops, but here again there is no way to positively attribute them to Coudersport without the background.)

234. Sock darner in end-of-day glass.

235. Tidbit dish in transparent green. The rim coloring is very similar to item 230. A Beitler contribution, it was also more than likely an experimental piece.

236. Morning Glory or trumpet-shaped whimsy in end-of-day glass. This one and item 238 make striking "take-home" whimsies, but they also fall into the same category as the long-handled sock darners. They can only be traced to a certain plant by having been passed down through the family of one of the workers. Even using this theory, there is room for error. Due to this difficulty, whimsies are not readily collected by people building a Coudersport glass collection.

237. Sock darner in end-of-day glass.

238. Morning Glory or trumpet-shaped whimsy in end-of-day glass.

ART GLASS VASES (PP. 64-68)

The Joseph Webb Decorative Glass Company and The Bastow Glass Company both produced beautiful vases using a wide assortment of glass and decorating methods.

The Coudersport Glass vases, as they have come to be known, were all mold blown and finished by hand. The vases shown in this section are all of the same style and were formed using the same size molds.

The diameter of these is 3.25" at the bottom. The top rim is flared out to various sizes ranging from 4" to 5.5" across. The height is determined by how much of the glass is pulled down in the flaring process. They are usually 11" to 11.5" tall.

The tri-cornered, petal-style top is another example of how this popular design was used at the Coudersport factory. The final product is a tall, graceful vase with simple but elegant lines. The thrill of finding their first vase of this style is a memory that collectors relive time and again. These vases still turn up at yard sales or estate auctions and are usually not identified as Coudersport Glass. This is what makes collecting such a joy!

PAGE 64

239. Opaque blue glass with a striking design of cattails, green leaves and an interesting butterfly. *(Museum Collection)*

240. Crystal vase with orange and white flowers using a simple dot and smudge style. This orange flower and the dot and smudge style of painting is used extensively on the pointed vases and water sets from Coudersport.

241. White opaline glass shading to custard. This glass is similar to the style of the Peachblow in the way the colors are worked together. This flower motif is used repeatedly on many decorated pieces at this factory. The painting here is done in a reverse fashion. The leaves painted in shades of brown form the outline of the flower which is the actual vase color showing through.

242. White opaline glass. The design has three birds perched on branches which have small flowers.

243. White opaline, no decoration. *(Museum Collection)*

244. Crystal, no decoration. *(Museum Collection)*

245. White opaline glass shading to a soft rose in the Peachblow style. A dog's head painted in brown is centered on the vase with a muted background. The detail of the dog is nicely done. A premium vase! *(Dehn Collection)*

PAGE 65

This page shows the wide range of color shades that were produced on the white opaline glass using rose or pink shading in the Peachblow style.

246. White opaline glass with a rose tint shading from dark at the top to light in the center and returning to dark at the base. *(Museum Collection)*

247. White opaline glass with true pink at the top quickly becoming almost completely white at the center, then turning to a light pink. The white is very evident at the base. *(Museum Collection)*

248. Pitcher made from the vase mold with an artistically styled applied handle. The white opaline glass has a deep pink tint in the top portion returning to white at the base. *(Museum Collection)*

249. White opaline glass with an all-over deep rose tint shading from dark rose on the top to a lighter shade in the center and returning to dark at the base. *(Author's Collection)*

250. White opaline glass with the top section of the vase in a shade of pink that has a strong tan cast. The lower area remains white. Quite different. *(Weimer Collection)*

251. White opaline glass with shades of brown painted in horizontal stripes in the area below the petals and at the base. Using the dot method, simple blue flowers are painted in the central area and at three places on the top surface. Top painting is unusual. *(Weimer Collection)*

252. White opaline glass with shades of vibrant true pink in the top portion and again at the base. The central area remains white. *(Weimer Collection)*

PAGE 66

A vibrant display of color is evident in this assortment of vases.

253. Transparent blue glass trimmed in gold. The design has a cluster of fern-style leaves growing upward toward a graceful dragonfly. *(Nelson Collection)*

254. Transparent cranberry glass. *(Museum Collection)*

255. White opaline glass attractively painted with the flower motif on an angle across the central section. The top rim of this vase has been fashioned in a jack-in-the-pulpit style, with the back up and the front down. Very rare. *(Thomas Collection)*

256. Transparent green glass trimmed in gold. The design has a cluster of fern-style leaves growing upward toward a dragonfly. *(Cooney Collection)*

257. Transparent green glass with orange and white flowers in the simple dot and smudge style. *(Museum Collection)*

258. Transparent blue glass.

259. Custard glass with tinted shadings, decorated with the flower decor in brown paint.

PAGE 67

The photograph on this page contains an array of opaque glass vases showing a variety of decorating styles.

260. Opaque white glass, undecorated, showing one petal shape turned upwards at a sharp angle with the tip actually turning in. *(Museum Collection)*

261. Opaline glass with yellow tints becoming lighter as it goes toward the base. Flower motif decoration done in more detail and over a larger area. *(Nelson Collection)*

262. Opaque glass mixed with shades of rose in the shiny Peachblow style.

263. Opaque white glass with shades of yellow. *(Museum Collection)*

264. Opaline glass with deep yellow tinting. The decoration is a head of a dog centered on a wispy background giving the allusion of smoke. Excellent detail painting. *(Museum Collection)*

265. Opaque blue glass with the flower motif painted in dark brown. Around this, there are added leaves or foliage in muted brown.

266. Opaque white glass with the fern design painted in gold.

Page 68

No numbered items. Descriptions included on page 68.

Water Sets (PP. 69-74)

The Joseph Webb Decorative Glass Company and The Bastow Glass Company both produced a varied selection of water sets using the mold-blown method. Sets of this type were very popular products and were made by many companies of this time period.

The identification of these are one of the most difficult tasks both Bob Currin and I are asked to do. Here again, we must remember that the men who made the molds, the glass blowers and the decorators all were noted for their habit of moving from place to place as work was available. Remember also, that this factory burned in 1904, and these men moved on and took there skills with them.

The pitchers are mold blown with smooth applied handles, and the tops are usually finished by hand. There has not been any evidence of a reeded or splined handle being made at the Coudersport plant. The goblets are molded and the top edges are finished on the better ones, though some are quite crudely done. Many of the goblets and some of the pitchers are paneled on the inside.

The water sets, or single pieces on the pages that follow, fall into two categories. The water sets that we have identified with shards or by other means are listed as category **A**. The other sets or items in this section are believed to be Coudersport pieces, but their attribution is less certain. I have put these in category **B**. As a collector of this glassware, one must often rely on instinct as there are no set rules to follow.

PAGE 69

267. Crystal glass pitcher, ball shape in the drape pattern. Top is formed into a modified petal shape. (A) *(Nelson Collection)*

268 & 269. Crystal glass water set with pitcher and six glasses. Pitcher is in one of the common shapes with scroll and daisy style decoration. Touches of orange are frequently used. The glasses are paneled on the inside and the edges are nicely finished. (A) *(Cooney Collection)*

270 & 271. Crystal glass water set with pitcher and four glasses. Pitcher is in one of the popular shapes with pinwheel and dot designed trim in white and orange. The top is fluted. (A) *(Museum Collection)*

PAGE 70

272 & 273. This water set has a tall tankard style pitcher and four gracefully shaped glasses. The transparent blue glass is decorated with flowers shaped similar to Columbine blossoms. The decorating on this set is expertly done in shades of pastels and gold. (A) *(Nelson Collection)*

274 & 275. This set is the same as Nos. 272 & 273 but in clear crystal glass. (A) *(Nelson Collection)*

276 & 277. Same as Nos. 272 & 273 but in cranberry glass. (A) *(Museum Collection)*

PAGE 71

278 & 279. Transparent green glass water set. Pitcher is in a graceful tankard style and the six tumblers all have inner panels. An aster style blossom is the focal point of the painted trim. Shades of orange, yellow and white are used with a touch of blue. (A)

280 & 281. Transparent blue pitcher and one glass. Same style and trim as Nos. 278 & 279. (A) *(Nelson Collection)*

PAGE 72

282 & 283. Transparent blue water set with pitcher and five glasses, all paneled inside. The decoration consists of artistic but simple details in gold, white and orange. Top of pitcher is fluted and rims of the glasses are finished. (B) *(Bruzzi Collection)*

284 & 285. Tankard style pitcher and one tumbler in crystal. Nicely done decorations in gold and pastels. (A) *(Fry Collection)*

286. Cranberry glass pitcher in an unusual shape, with fluted top and applied crystal handle. Inside panels are apparent in lower section. Predominately white and gold decorations. Donated to the Potter County Historical Society Museum by the family of a worker from the Coudersport factory. (A)

287 & 288. Unusual tankard style pitcher and three glasses. Deep transparent green glass with a geometric style decoration in white and gold. These pieces were also given to the museum from an area family. (A)

289. Transparent green pitcher with fluted top and painted trim using the smudge and dot style. Pastel colors. (A) *(Museum Collection)*

PAGE 73

290 & 291. Pitcher and four tumblers in dark amethyst. This water set is the same style as Nos. 268 & 269. The design has the orange scrolls and small blue dot style flowers. Inner paneling is evident. (A) *(Museum Collection)*

292 & 293. Pitcher and four tumblers are from the same molds as Nos. 290 & on the top of this page. The only difference is that this pitcher has a plain top. The painting is in gold and pastels with orange centers on the flowers. (B)

294 & 295. Dark amethyst pitcher and four tumblers. The rim of the pitcher shows an edge treatment very similar to the Trailing Vine line. Details of the decoration include the same five petaled flower used on the Coudersport vases and other trimmed items. (B) *(Weimer Collection)*

PAGE 74

296. Crystal glass pitcher in the same pattern as No. 289. Trimmed with the dot & smudge style above an arrangement of blue asters. (A) *(Museum Collection)*

297. Crystal pitcher with a fluted top. The decoration on this piece is very finely painted and includes some interesting leaves done with dots. (A) *(Museum Collection)*

298. Tall tankard pitcher in a bulged-out style. Crystal glass with an attractive tulip decoration. (A) *(Museum Collection)*

299. Six crystal tumblers with inside paneling and an orange and white floral design on a washed blue background. (B)

300. This beautiful opalescent drape pattern pitcher is at The Potter County Historical Society Museum. The corresponding shards are also there. The fluted top has a white opalescent edge heavily flared and crimped. The graceful drape is accented by the light opalescence. A real beauty. (A) *(Museum Collection)*

301. Pair of crystal tumblers decorated with a smudge-style stripe on an angle and a stem of small flowers. (B) *(Museum Collection)*

THIS 'N THAT (P. 75)

302. This wonderful whimsy is made in the shape of a miniature oil lamp. Using a custard mustard jar, the creative glassworker has added a flared chimney. This 'take-home' piece is only 4" high and the top shade flares out to a 2.5" diameter. This darling lamp is owned by one of the first avid bottle diggers from our area, Rayburn (Jaybird) Weimer.

303. When a large collection of Coudersport glass was sold, this pitcher was included. Whether it is Coudersport or not remains to be seen. The opaque blue glass is identical to the opaque blue from this company. The applied handle matches others in this book and the top is crudely finished.

304. This beautiful pitcher has not been completely identified as Coudersport, primarily because the shape is different. However, the transparent green matches other pieces and the painting has a strong resemblance to other designs, so it is quite possible that this shape was made at Coudersport. *(Nelson Collection)*

305. This attractive vase was given to the museum by the Beitler family. There can be no doubt that Mr. Beitler did the decorating, but was it actually molded in Coudersport? There have been no other examples of this shape found. *(Museum Collection)*

306 & 307. Like No. 304, this amethyst tumbler and pitcher cannot be positively identified as Coudersport. The pitcher has the same shape as No. 304, and the decoration resembles work done at Coudersport. *(Leete Collection)*

308 & 309. This set is also hard to identify. The shape is different from any other; the tint in the transparent green glass is different, and the handle is applied much higher and is an entirely different shape. On the other hand, the formation of the top is the same, the painting is similar and paneling is evident in the pitcher. This water set has a history of coming from an area family that had a worker at the plant. *(Peet Collection)*

310 & 311. I am picturing the Three Fingers & Panel spooner from page 59 beside a sugar bowl base for comparison. Note the difference in the diameter of the pedestal bases. The sugar bowl diameter is 3.812" while the spooner is only 3". This view also clearly shows the lip to hold the lid. I also want to point out the attractive gold trim on the sugar bowl. Surely Harry Bastow had plans to enlarge upon this line. Due to the scarcity of this pattern, the damage is overlooked by the owner until a perfect replacement can be found. *(Peet Collection)*

312. This is a beautiful Bride's Basket, but was it made in Coudersport? I doubt it. The mold is different from the other Bride's Baskets. The perfect fluting of the rim with the added crystal edge and the quilted effect in the bowl are not consistent with Coudersport Glass. Since this came from the Beitler family, it is apparent that the painting was done by Mr. Beitler using his five petaled flower decor, but I have to assume that this was done after he left Coudersport. *(Museum Collection)*

WINE SETS (P. 76)

In December of 1903, *China, Glass & Lamps* reported, "The Bastow Glass Company at Coudersport, Pa., expect to make pressed pitchers, wine sets and novelties in the future."

On May 9, 1903, the Coudersport Seventh Day Adventist Church was organized. The Communion Set shown here was purchased at the Bastow Glass Company by C.V. McVagh for the use of the charter members at the inaugural communion service. The set consists of the wine decanter and a small goblet for use by the men and an identical goblet for women.

The original church was located on Chestnut Street in Coudersport. When the new building on South Main Street was constructed, a place of honor in the entrance hall was built to display this communion set.

The church officials were very accommodating when I asked for permission to have the photography done. Thanks to this wonderful gesture, this piece of Coudersport glass history can now be recorded for future generations.

313. Pair of small wine goblets in transparent green decorated in gold and white. The popular dot method of painting has been used with extreme care. The inside of the bowls are paneled. Approximately 4" high.

314. Wine decanter with applied handle. Like the goblets, the transparent green glass is decorated in gold and white. The interior is paneled and the spout is the tri-cornered petal design. Approximately 10" high.

315 & 316. Wine decanter and wine goblet. This set is in the same style as the communion set above, though it was formed in a different mold. It is also made in transparent green glass but has pastel and gold decorations. The formation of the spout and the handle are identical. The panels on the interior form a subdued star in the base. (Many pitchers from this plant have a similar star effect.) The larger flower decoration is the same as on other Coudersport items. However, the goblet is heavier and a different shape. It appears to be a later style, which provides a good example of the dilemmas a Coudersport Glass collector faces.

Canes and Chain (P. 77)

The glassblowers of the early 1900's used the glass left at the end of the day to make whimsy or "take-home" items. These were not production pieces. The positive identification of the origin of the various whimsies is next to impossible. The canes and the chain shown on this page are reputed to have been made at the Bastow Glass Company.

317-320. Glass canes in various colors. Different techniques have been used to achieve some unique and striking items. These canes were often carried by glassworkers while marching in Labor Day parades. All canes are from the *Peet Collection.*

321. Crystal glass chain with a heart and loop design. A lot of time and ingenuity went into this marvelous creation. (To display this chain we have used a substitute for the one link missing on the left.) *(Leete Collection)*

Stag & Holly, Reproductions, and More (PP. 78-80)

Shown in the first photo are two items from the Beitler family. These are products from other companies decorated by Mr. Beitler. Since these are in the historical society, I am showing them here to clear up any misunderstandings.

The two views of the Stag & Holly reproduction bowl that is being made today are included on page 80 for the reader's benefit. Whether you maintain that the Stag & Holly is Coudersport or Fenton, you need to be aware of these. See also the comments by James Measell on page 78.

The new bowls are much heavier, almost to the point of feeling clumsy. The rim edge is very square and much thicker than the originals. The transparent green and pink glass is very close to the shades of the earlier ones.

The Basketweave condiment set shown at the top right on page 80 is an example of the sets that have been made in Japan. These are produced in cased glass in various colors that are obviously from a later period. The original sets were all opaque glass. As far as I can determine, there was no cased glass made in Coudersport. The base is the same size as the original but it is much heavier. The chrome-plated handle has the top ring hanging from the upright as opposed to the formed ring on the original.

The salt and pepper shakers in this reproduction set are the same size as the mustard pot. The Coudersport Basketweave shakers measure 1.0625" in diameter across the threads, while mustards measure 1.5" at the threads. If you stand a shaker beside a mustard, the roping at the top of the caning will be about one eighth inch higher on the shaker. These reproduction shakers and mustards all have nicely finished rims, not the rough rims of the original pieces. The tops are chrome plated with a point in the center.

This Japanese set is white opaque glass with an overlay of amber glass. I have seen this same set in a shade of green that reminded me of the old avocado color.

Photo Credits

Curt Weinhold—page 33 (lower), 34, 38, 43 (row 1), 43 (rows 2 & 3), 46, 48 (row 1), 52 (rows 2 & 3), 54, 56 (row 2), 58 (row 2), 68, 72 (nos. 282 & 283), 76, 78, 80 (top row, right).

David Richardson—page 33 (top), 35, 36, 39, 40, 41, 42, 43 (rows 2 & 3), 44 (row 3), 45, 47, 48 (rows 2 & 3), 49, 50, 51, 52 (row 1), 53, 55, 56 (row 1), 57, 58 (rows 1 & 3), 59, 60, 61, 62, 63, 64, 65, 66, 67, 69, 70, 71, 72 (nos. 284-289), 73, 74, 75, 76 (rows 2 & 3), 77, 80 (row 1 left & rows 2 & 3).

The Trailing Vine Creamer (page 30) was sketched by Christina Colucci while she was an intern at the Pennsylvania Lumber Museum, Galeton, Pennsylvania.

Credits

Sincere thanks to these collectors who loaned pictures and/or items to be photographed for this book:

(Bruzzi) Scott Bruzzi

(Buchsen) Paul and Delores Buchsen

(Cooney) Mina Cooney

(Darrin) Ed and Tess Darrin

(Dehn) Jackie Dehn

(Fry) Martin and Sarah Fry

(Leete) Tom and Shirlee Leete

(Nelson) Janice and Curtis Nelson

(Peet) John and Carlene Peet

(Roberts) Carl and Linda Roberts

(Thomas) Jim and Penny Thomas

(Weimer) Raymond (Jaybird) and Esther Weimer

Bibliography

Archives, Potter County Court House, Coudersport, Pennsylvania.
(Fire settlement information).

Archives, Potter County Historical Society, Main Street, Coudersport, Pennsylvania.

Archives, *Potter County Journal* (newspaper), Coudersport, Pennsylvania.

Archives & Microfilm, *Potter Enterprise* (newspaper), Coudersport, Pennsylvania.

Bliss, Floyd W. "Art Glass & Pressed Glass Made by the Coudersport Tile and
Ornamental Glass Co." *The Spinning Wheel* (November 1972).

China, Glass & Lamps (trade journal), 1900-1904.

China Glass & Pottery Review (trade journal), 1900-1904.

Commoner & Glassworker (trade journal), Pittsburgh, Pennsylvania, 1900-1903.

Edwards, Bill. *Standard Encyclopedia of Opalescent Glass.* Paducah, Kentucky:
Collector Books, 1995.

Heacock, William. *Encyclopedia of Victorian Colored Pattern Glass, Book II,
Opalescent Glass from A to Z.* Marietta, Ohio: Antique Publications, 1975.

Heacock, William. *Encyclopedia of Victorian Colored Pattern Glass, Book 4, Custard
Glass from A to Z.* Marietta, Ohio: Antique Publications, 1976.

Lechner, Mildred & Ralph. *The World of Salt Shakers.* Paducah, Kentucky: Collector
Books, 1992.

Personal study and interviews. The Fenton Art Glass Company, Williamstown,
West Virginia.

Personal study and interviews. The Rakow Library, Corning Museum of Glass,
Corning, New York.

Photo Morgue. *Leader Enterprise* (newspaper). Coudersport, Pennsylvania.

Storey, Helen. "The Problem of Rush Bases." National Milk Glass Collector's Society,
Opaque News, Vol. 4, No. 1 (December 1988), pp. 409-410.

The Agitator (newspaper). Wellsboro, Pennsylvania, c. 1900.

On the Cover

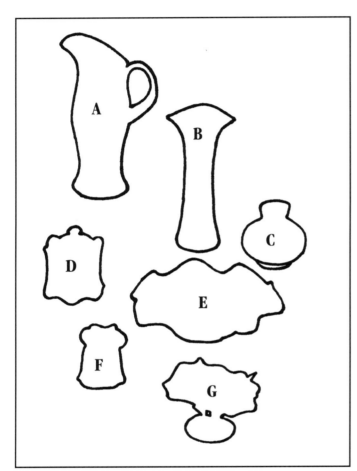

Pieces are described and identified by the item numbers used in the book.

FRONT COVER:

A. Decorated pitcher in cranberry glass (277)

B. Custard vase (259)

C. Water jug (220)

D. Transparent green, gold decorated covered sugar (106)

E. Bride's Basket (215)

F. Vaseline opalescent novelty (143)

G. Waffle & Vine compote (211)

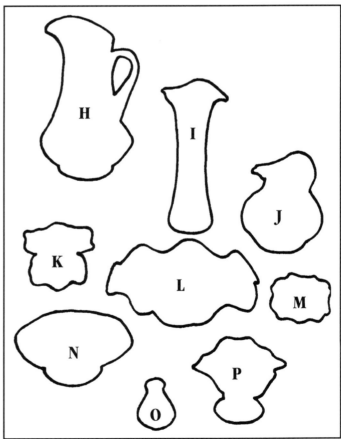

BACK COVER:

H. Decorated tankard pitcher (279)

I. Decorated vase (245)

J. Pompeii ware (226)

K. Ladies spittoon (37)

L. Bride's Basket (217)

M. Trailing Vine berry bowl (118)

N. Base of a butter dish in custard glass (208)

O. Fantasia shaker, new top (227)

P. Waffle & Vine compote (212)

2000 Value Guide

The following values have been derived from the most recent sales, personal experience, and the use of information from other collectors. I have taken into consideration the fact that this book identifies Coudersport Glass for a new realm of collectors. The opalescent, vaseline, custard and opaque glass collectors, as well as the art glass community, now have a new field of items to search out.

The price estimates listed below are only a guide. There is bound to be a lot of pros and cons concerning these values. Whether you agree or disagree, please keep in mind that this is the first complete attempt to put values on Coudersport Glass.

The values are for glassware in mint condition unless stated otherwise in the description. Neither the author nor the publisher can be held liable for losses incurred by those using this price guide as the basis for any sale or other transaction.

1. 40-50	**20.** 115-135	**38.** 100-110	**56.** 60-70
2. 35-40	**21.** 125-150	**39.** 325-350	**57.** 200-225
3. 25-30	**22.** 275-325	**40.** 90-115	**58.** 60-70
4. 40-50	**23.** 100-125	**41.** 90-115	**59.** 60-70
5. 35-40	**24.** 325-350	**42.** 110-125	**60.** 60-70
6. 25-30	**25.** 110-125	**43.** 50-65	**61.** 75-80
7. 25-30	**26.** 115-125	**44.** 50-65	**62.** 60-70
8. 25-30	**27.** 50-65	**45.** 200-225	**63.** 75-85
9. 25-30	**28.** 90-115	**46.** 50-65	**64.** 350-375
10. 100-125	**29.** 50-65	**47.** 50-65	**65.** 475-500
11. 110-135	**30.** 200-225	**48.** 100-110	**66.** 550-575
12. 130-135	**31.** 60-70	**49.** 85-95	**67.** 375-400
13. 120-145	**32.** 80-90	**50.** 80-95	**68.** 125-140
14. 100-125	**33.** 80-90	**51.** 225-235	**69.** 115-130
15. 90-115	**34.** 75-80	**51A.** 475-500	**70.** 115-130
16. 110-130	**35.** 225-235	**52.** 220-230	**71.** 125-140
17. 120-145	**35A.** 450-475	**53.** 345-355	**72.** 100-120
18. 90-115	**36.** 90-110	**54.** 200-225	**73.** 350-375
19. 125-150	**37.** 425-475	**55.** 125-130	**74.** 300-350

75. 140-160	**108.** 110-130	**141.** 125-140	**174.** 50-55
76. 365-380	**109.** 120-145	**142.** 125-140	**175.** 50-55
77. 395-410	**110.** 85-110	**143.** 125-150	**176.** 50-55
78. 140-160	**111.** 110-130	**144.** 110-120	**177.** 50-55
79. 75-85	**112.** 135-145	**145.** 100-110	**178.** 100-110
80. 235-250	**113.** 75-90	**146.** 100-110	**179.** 200 pair
81. 200-220	**114.** 250-270	**147.** 100-110	**180.** 200 pair
82. 130-140	**115.** 85-110	**148.** 100-110	**181.** 110-120
83. 85-90	**116.** 125-140	**149.** 125-140	**182.** 115-125
84. 85-90	**117.** 300-320	**150.** 125-150	**183.** 130-140
85. 110-120	**118.** 125-140	**151.** 125-140	**184.** 100-110
86. 145-160	**119.** 150-160	**152.** 100-120	**185.** 125-135
87. 400-435	**120.** 100-125	**153.** 125-145	**186.** 100-110
88. 150-160	**121.** 250-270	**154.** 60-70	**187.** 100-110
89. 100-125	**122.** 100-125	**155.** 60-70	**188.** 110-120
90. 200-225	**123.** 200-215	**156.** 60-70	**189.** 110-120
91. 50-60	**124.** 200-215	**157.** 60-70	**190.** 95-105
92. 225-235	**125.** 225-240	**158.** 60-70	**191.** 120-130
93. 110-125	**126.** 125-130	**159.** 60-70	**192.** 110-120
94. 250-300	**127.** 400-425	**160.** 60-70	**193.** 100-110
95. 110-125	**128.** 125-130	**161.** 60-70	**194.** 125-135
96. 325-350	**129.** 100-110	**162.** 60-70	**195.** 175-200
97. 40-50	**130.** 110-120	**163.** 60-70	**196.** 135-145
98. 85-110	**131.** 100-110	**164.** 60-70	**197.** 100-110
99. 50-55	**132.** 100-110	**165.** 60-70	**198.** 100-110
100. 100-110	**133.** 100-110	**166.** 60-70	**199.** 175-200
101. 40-50	**134.** 100-110	**167.** 65-70	**200.** 175-200
102. 45-60	**135.** 100-110	**168.** 65-70	**201.** 25-30
103. 90-100	**136.** 230-240	**169.** 65-70	**202.** 25-30
104. 200-215	**137.** 100-110	**170.** 50-55	**203.** 35-45
105. 395-425	**138.** 125-140	**171.** 50-55	**204.** 35-45
106. 375-400	**139.** 135-155	**172.** 50-55	**205.** 395-425
107. 110-130	**140.** 125-140	**173.** 50-55	**206.** 225-275

207. 395-425	**236.** 150-175	**265.** 225-250	**294.** 85-110
208. 120-125	**237.** 150-175	**266.** 215-240	**295.** 130-150
209. 350-375	**238.** 150-175	**267.** 150-175	**296.** 125-150
210. 225-275	**239.** 225-250	**268.** 100-135	**297.** 125-150
211. 475-525	**240.** 200-225	**269.** 125-150	**298.** 135-150
212. 475-525	**241.** 225-250	**270.** 125-150	**299.** 110-135
213. 475-525	**242.** 225-250	**271.** 85-100	**300.** 165-190
214. 475-525	**243.** 200-225	**272.** 110-125	**301.** 65-85
215. 230-250	**244.** 175-200	**273.** 175-195	**302.** 175-200
216. 185-220	**245.** 400-450	**274.** 110-125	**303.** 95-110
217. 185-220	**246.** 375-400	**275.** 175-195	**304.** 125-150
218. 185-220	**247.** 375-400	**276.** 110-125	**305.** 95-110
219. 230-250	**248.** 325-350	**277.** 175-195	**306.** 25-30
220. 500-525	**249.** 375-400	**278.** 125-150	**307.** 125-150
221. 475-520	**250.** 375-400	**279.** 175-200	**308.** 25-30
222. 475-520	**251.** 200-220	**280.** 25-35	**309.** 125-150
223. 500-525	**252.** 375-400	**281.** 125-150	**310.** 225-275
224. 200-250	**253.** 200-225	**282.** 100-125	**311.** 95-105
225. 200-230	**254.** 175-225	**283.** 130-150	*(damaged)*
226. 200-250	**255.** 250-275	**284.** 20-35	**312.** 95-115
227. 175-200	**256.** 200-225	**285.** 125-145	**313.** 75-85
228. 175-200	**257.** 200-225	**286.** 125-150	**314.** 175-200
229. 150-180	**258.** 175-200	**287.** 65-75	**315.** 25-30
230. 175-200	**259.** 225-250	**288.** 125-145	**316.** 95-115
231. 200-250	**260.** 200-225	**289.** 125-150	**317.** 200-250
232. 150-175	**261.** 235-255	**290.** 85-110	**318.** 165-185
233. 150-200	**262.** 375-400	**291.** 125-150	**319.** 200-250
234. 150-175	**263.** 210-235	**292.** 125-150	**320.** 250-275
235. 175-200	**264.** 375-400	**293.** 85-110	**321.** 200-225

Notes